BLACK
PEARLS

ALSO BY ERIC V. COPAGE

*Kwanzaa: An African-American Celebration
of Culture and Cooking*

Black Pearls for Parents

Black Pearls Journal

A Kwanzaa Fable

BLACK PEARLS

Daily Meditations,
Affirmations,
and Inspirations for
African-Americans

Eric V. Copage

Amistad
An Imprint of HarperCollinsPublishers

HarperCollins books may be purchased for educational, business, or sales promotional use. For information, please write:
Special Markets Department, HarperCollins Publishers Inc.,
10 East 53rd Street, New York, NY 10022.

Originally published in 1993 by Quill/William Morrow
and Company.

FIRST AMISTAD EDITION PUBLISHED IN 2004.

Designed by Michael Mendelsohn

Printed on acid-free paper

Library of Congress Cataloging-in-Publication Data
Copage, Eric V.
Black pearls : daily meditations, affirmations, and inspirations for African-Americans / by Eric V. Copage.
p. cm.
ISBN 0-688-12291-4
1. Afro-Americans—Life skills guides. I. Title.
E185.86.C588 1993   92-33186
158'.1'08996073—dc20   CIP

20 QUADM 70 69 68 67

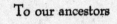

To our ancestors

To our ancestors

INTRODUCTION

As a child growing up in Los Angeles, I was always intrigued by my grandmother's pocketbook-sized Bible, which she kept in a purse and carried with her everywhere. I noticed how she would begin her days with a quote from one of the Gospels, or rejuvenate herself throughout the day by reading an inspirational section of the Old Testament. I envied the confidence and peace she gained from those words. As I grew older, I began to think: Wouldn't it be great for black Americans to have such a book? Not a religious book, but a book of inspiring sayings and practical advice that stemmed specifically from *our* heritage and *our* people. Wouldn't it be great, I thought, for those of us of African descent to have a small book of meditations, affirmations, and inspirations, derived from our culture, with which we could start the day or which we could use anytime to jolt flagging spirits or boost self-confidence.

Black Pearls is intended to be such a book. In it I hope to impart lessons and pearls of wisdom that give full expression to the diversity of our African-American heritage. The 365 quotes that begin each day's entry range from African proverbs and great sayings of Frederick Douglass and Sojourner Truth to wisdom from contemporary African-Americans including Terry McMillan, Eldridge Cleaver, Oprah Winfrey, Quincy Jones, Muhammad Ali, Bill Cosby, Jamaica Kincaid, and many others. From these daily inspirations, I've suggested meditations and specific daily actions. Each day covers a new topic: self-determination, heritage, affirmative action, love, dieting, victimhood, power and success, to name just a few. Like a cup of coffee in the morning, beginning the day with one of the book's meditations can brace one for the day's activities.

While reading *Black Pearls*, you might want to remember that I have used the long-standing social definition (there is no "scientific" definition) of who is black, namely, that any amount of African heritage means that you are black. Also, when I refer to children in the book I'm not just talking about biological children, but about African-American youngsters in general.

I have emphasized visualization because it has been shown, through experiments with athletes, that the focused, relaxed mind going over a task paves the way for accomplishing that task in real life. And because it's important not to obsess over an object or an event, I have usually suggested spending only five minutes on an exercise.

Some exercises recur periodically throughout the book because some things—working toward one's goals, for instance—require repetition throughout the year to be successful. And, speaking of "goals," you will notice that it is probably *the* most common word in this book. Just remember that when I refer to "goals," I mean anything *you* might want to accomplish—from being a better automobile driver to making the perfect cherry pie! "Goals" should not be taken as referring exclusively to professional ambitions. Last, if you don't know a person I have quoted, use this as an opportunity to go to the library and look him or her up!

To be black in America is to be marked and differentiated like no other group in American society. This is not a complaint, just a fact. For centuries our skin color, hair texture, and facial features have marked us as a people held in bondage, and even after emancipation, we have been marked for rare virulence in ongoing discrimination.

But as we continue our struggle, each and

every one of us—through Unity, Self-Determination, Collective Work and Responsibility, Cooperative Economics, Creativity, Purpose, and Faith—will look at our heritage and decide what it will mean—not to other ethnic groups, but to ourselves. There is a growing movement to make what once marked us negatively become our stamp of personal and collective excellence. I hope this book contributes to that movement.

—ERIC V. COPAGE

BLACK
PEARLS

FAITH

*I've had so many downs that I knew the law of
averages would be in my favor one day.*

—Doug Williams

When life seems to bring nothing but a string of
defeats and disappointments, we've got to have faith
that something good is still in store for us. With this
faith, we can forge ahead and continue to put forth
our best effort. Without it, we give up and accept
what comes our way, good or bad. Our precious
dreams begin to seem absurdities.

It is imperative that we see ourselves as worthy
and deserving of a good life. There may be rejections;
it may take us a while; but as long as we stay in the
game, there's every chance we'll score. On the side-
lines, we can only watch as others do the work and
the winning.

*On this day, I will spend five minutes to relax and
visualize success in achieving one of my goals.*

PLANNING

I don't like short-term solutions; they can come back and bite you in the behind later.

—Caroline R. Jones

Sometimes short-term solutions are necessary. A bit of fast and fancy footwork can get this month's rent or tuition paid, or a school or work assignment turned in on time. But a lifetime of close calls is stressful and fatiguing. Time spent constantly scrambling to meet our deadlines can deplete us of energy better applied to pursuing our dreams and enjoying our lives.

What do we need to do to make our lives easier, more manageable? Let's do some planning. The quick fix may serve to get us through a crisis, but crises recur when the underlying cause is not addressed.

On this day, I will take five minutes to write down one of my goals and devise a long-term strategy as to how to accomplish that goal.

HERITAGE

For us, Africa is not so much a lost continent
as an imagined one.

—JACK E. WHITE

There is irony in the fact that many of us are home-sick for a place we really do not know. It rests with us to learn about the birthplace of our ancestors.

We should all know, for example, about the Kingdoms of Ghana, Songhay, and Mali. We are enriched when we study the complex religious heritage and philosophy of life of African peoples—among them the Yoruba and the Kongo.

Let us go beyond our kente cloth ties and hats to learn of our heritage before our people were chained and brought here. Our culture was stripped from and denied our enslaved ancestors, but *we* are able and morally bound to pick it up again.

On this day, I will take five minutes to meditate
upon something I have that reminds me of my
African descent—it may be a piece of African cloth, a
sculpture, a family photograph—and let it inspire me
to learn more about Africa and do the best I can in
whatever I have to accomplish today.

January 3

ASSERTIVENESS

*I made speech my birthright ... talking back
became for me a rite of initiation.*

—BELL HOOKS

We all need to "talk back" once in a while, in our
own style. Going through life we may encounter a
number of people who will try to pin the blame on
us for their errors or shortcomings. We need to stand
up for ourselves in such cases and refuse to be the
scapegoat.

For some of us, this may go against the grain;
we don't like to appear strident or defensive. But if we
sit there and take it, our inner rage builds. Why carry
that around with us, or risk taking it out indirectly on
innocent people? We may be angry, but we needn't
be gratuitous or vituperative in our "back talk"; we
ought to be smart about what we're saying and how
we say it. But remember, there is no glory or saintli-
ness in being the long-suffering victim of abuse.

*On this day, I will take five minutes to remember a
day when I was challenged, or wrongly accused, and
will imagine myself "talking back," standing up for
myself in a forceful and effective manner.*

RENEWAL

When things got bad, I'd just sing "Ave Maria," which is one of my favorite songs from childhood . . . it was my salvation. It gave me a reason to believe that things would change.

—AARON NEVILLE

All of us, being human, have times that are awfully difficult. We are challenged in all sorts of ways—poverty, failed love (both familial and romantic), addictions.

Some find spiritual sustenance in a song, in poetry, art, nature, or in their children. Others find it in church or through prayer. We should know what works for us, what brings us through our worst moments and renews our conviction that life is worth living, that things will improve.

On this day, I will take five minutes to reflect upon what gives my life meaning. I will remember to use this song, line of poetry, or comforting image to help renew my strength when I am in despair or when I need inspiration to go on fighting.

CHILDHOOD

. . . they'll probably talk about my hard childhood and never understand that all the while I was quite happy.

—*NIKKI GIOVANNI*

Few of us might describe our childhoods as ideal or perfect. Perhaps money was tight and we never went on vacation, or we were embarrassed by our second-hand clothes.

Still, there are the little things we can find happiness in.

We can all reach back to summon up those delicious memories of childhood. Maybe it was the way Mother shampooed our hair that felt so good, or the times Dad played ball with us after dinner, or Grandma's peach pies, or going to church at Christmas.

Out of these memories, we see that life is made up of little things that may get lost when we only see the Big Picture.

On this day, I will take five minutes to remember a pleasant sensation from my childhood: a memorable and pleasant sight, sound, or touch.

SELF-RELIANCE

Self-help is the best help.
—AESOP, *from "Hercules and the Wagoner"*

Surely no truth could be plainer to African-Americans than this. Otherwise, we'd still be waiting for our forty acres and a mule.

How sad to sit back and expect others to fix our problems. That gives them all the power, and leaves us as beggars, palms outstretched.

When we help ourselves, we empower ourselves. We are active, not passive, and our efforts generate the energy to do more. We teach our children, our friends and neighbors that they, too, are in control, able to live full and meaningful lives.

On this day, I will sit down and think of five things I can do to bring me nearer to one of my life's goals.

January 7

HARMONY

If we do not work at releasing the inharmonious thoughts and attitudes that grow deep within, there is nothing that mere physical release can do for us.

—JULIETTE MCGINNIS, *stress management therapist*

Making a commitment to spend more time at the gym can do wonders for our muscle tone and cardiovascular endurance. It can even help reduce our levels of stress—in the short term. But if we expect a workout to give an overhaul to our mental outlook, we set ourselves up for disappointment.

No distraction or quick fix can address the real issues that plague us and keep us from feeling good about ourselves and our lives. When we cling to ancient hurts, anger, self-doubts, and other negative emotions and attitudes, we experience life with a clouded vision of what it has to offer.

It may take a while, and some practice, to let go of our pessimism. We'll have to nudge ourselves when we find we're falling into old habits.

I pledge to take five minutes at the end of this day and look for at least one good thing that happened to me.

BEGINNING

The first thing I typed was my name.
I wanted to see how it looked in print.
Then I began to type my poems.

—AUGUST WILSON

If you have never personally known an individual who has later acquired incredible fame and success, perhaps you have found yourself looking hard at early photos of, say, Muhammad Ali or Althea Gibson, or Kareem Abdul Jabar. We look to see if we can discern something of the greatness they later achieved. Or perhaps we visualize the first time August Wilson sat at a typewriter.

All great accomplishment begins somewhere. There are lost fights, missed shots, contrived poems. The important thing is that there is a beginning.

We must allow ourselves the opportunity to make our starts. Some may be false starts; we may lose interest in an endeavor. But another start might be the beginning of greatness or of self-fulfillment. We are entitled. Let's not be afraid to make a start. *On this day, I will take one concrete action—write a letter, make a call, look up an article—to start myself toward accomplishing a goal.*

RELAXATION

*I couldn't figure out why I was tired . . . why
all these people kept saying they had a hard
time catching up with me and, eventually,
stopped trying.*

—NTOZAKE SHANGE

There are times in our lives when we realize we've
overextended ourselves. Commitments to work and
family, to school, church, and to friends build up to
the point where we suddenly find ourselves overwhelmed. Some people make a habit of living this
way, filling up every blank space on their calendars.

Well, a full life doesn't have to mean a hectic
life. Time to relax and be introspective, to enjoy our
children, to read a book or go for a walk in the park,
helps us maintain a balance in our lives.

We may need to be more selective about the
commitments we undertake and to realize that saying
no to some allows us to concentrate more fully on
those we say yes to.

*On this day, I will take five minutes to be in total
silence and passively observe and note the images that
float before my mind's eye.*

DIETING/LOVE

When I fell in love, I'd lose weight and then
when the relationship failed, I'd gain it back.
Food and heartache are intertwined within me.
—*Luther Vandross*

With many of us, food is intertwined with all sorts
of emotions. We are sad or nervous, frustrated or
empty inside, and we seek the comfort of food. We
are elated and in celebratory spirits, and we reward
ourselves with a delicious treat.

When food (or cigarettes, alcohol, or drugs)
becomes our adult pacifier, we have a problem. We
need to know that food cannot fill the void inside us
or relieve our stress. It cannot make up for love lost
or thwarted ambitions. When we look to food in difficult times, we actually create a new problem for
ourselves: unhealthy dependency. A weight gain
makes plain our lack of control and diminishes our
self-esteem. Feeling down, we eat more and the cycle
continues. Let us leave food to nourish and delight
us, the things it does best.

On this day, I pledge that if I find myself in a funk,
I will determine what could make me feel better
without hurting me at the same time.

OPTIMISM

I want to see how life can triumph.

—ROMARE BEARDEN

Keeping a positive attitude is no easy task. It seems we are constantly challenged. If we're not careful, we may come to view life as a succession of pits and hurdles, alternately threatening to entrap us or bring us down groaning.

Fortunately, the human spirit is strong and gets stronger still after each hurdle successfully cleared, each pit deftly crossed or escaped. Triumph fortifies us to face the future. Pessimism is a killer and must be swept out the door, so that optimism can find a welcome home in our lives. Let's praise ourselves so that we *expect* to win.

On this day, I will take five minutes to remember winning something, and I will re-experience the sounds, sights, and feelings of that victory.

January 12

INDEPENDENCE

Being your own man does not mean taking advantage of anyone else.

—FLIP WILSON

We cannot acquire maturity and responsibility if we are constantly relying on parents, a spouse, or friends. The young woman with no plans for the future who has her mother raise her child and the man who always borrows money from friends without focusing on how to repay them are both dependent until they take control of their lives. We must guard against opting for the easy way out. Then we can stand tall.

On this day, I will take five minutes to wonder if there has been any person I have leaned on too much. If so, I will resolve to think of a way to become more independent. If I cannot think of someone, I will congratulate myself.

PURPOSE

*The dog has four feet, but he does not walk
them in four roads.*

—*HAITIAN proverb*

When moving toward our goals, we do well to concentrate our efforts. That's not to say we shouldn't
have alternate paths in mind in case the one we're
on turns out to be a dead end. Sometimes we find
ourselves working one job while trying to get our own
projects or business going. Life can be a scramble.

Nevertheless, let's focus our efforts on what's
most important. If one of our ideas seems promising
and about ready to hatch, we can buckle down to it.

*On this day, I will take five minutes to write out my
various goals and decide, in order of importance,
which ones I should pay most attention to.*

January 14

COLLECTIVE RESPONSIBILITY

We rarely goes down by ourse'fs.
—JOHN JASPER

In a concrete way, most of us are directly responsible to others—children, parents, mates, or spouses. When we cease to function as productive, responsible adults, it is not just we who suffer. While mates or spouses, parents or friends, can disassociate themselves from our harmful ways, children seldom have that opportunity. How sad for them to be dragged down into our misery.

That is why we must make it a priority to stay mentally and spiritually healthy. Allowing ourselves to be seduced by reckless behavior and destructive people or vices is a choice *we* make. It's within our power to live healthily; it's our duty to ourselves to do so.

In living up to our personal responsibilities, we strengthen our family and our community. We are examples of quiet heroism to all around us.

On this day, I will do something for an African-American colleague, friend, acquaintance, or family member. I might simply express happiness that he or she is around and part of my life.

COURAGE

*The higher the monkey climbs, the more it is
exposed to danger.*

—*BELIZEAN proverb*

It may seem that the higher we go, the farther we
have to fall. What we may not consider, however, is
that there are an awful lot of branches to grab on to
on the way down. As long as we reach for them, we
may not fall all the way to the ground.

Let's not permit the height of our ambitions
to deter us from climbing as far as we'd like to go.
If we falter at the top and drop down a little, we can
always find another branch—perhaps a sturdier
one—to reach for and pull ourselves up again.

*On this day, I will take another step toward
accomplishing one of my goals.*

GOD

*People see God every day; they just don't
recognize Him.*

—PEARL BAILEY

How we see God affects the way we live our lives. If
God is the angry power who censures and punishes
us, we probably live with fear and anxiety. We may
toe the line and be resentful, or cross the line to spite
a God we consider cruel and unjust. Not a pleasant
way to spend our time on earth. If, however, we recognize that God is in all of us, then we can start to
treat ourselves and our brothers and sisters with
respect.

Many walk among us who are out of touch
with their spiritual selves, who would be baffled by
such a notion as God within us. Can life then have
much value? We are quick to spot the devil in us,
why not the divine? It is the light within that can
light our lives and light our way.

*On this day, I will take five quiet minutes to
recognize the divine in me, and to remember that
through me the divine manifests itself in the world.*

January 17

SELF-DETERMINATION

The adults in my life told me I could do anything if I was determined and resourceful. . . . I was expected to be ambitious because there was an intrinsic pleasure in excelling, not because I had to prove anything to whites.

—ERIC V. COPAGE

It's difficult, if not impossible, to prove anything to a bigot because he has already committed his mind to a particular viewpoint. Why waste time and energy focusing on the expectations of anyone but ourselves?

We need to be in command of our lives and put aside the expectations or doubts of others. Let's excel because it feels good. There is personal joy in accomplishment; it adds meaning to our lives.

On this day, I will take five minutes to think about the course I would like my life to take.

SPACE

*There are periods when I am the most attentive
and thoughtful lover in the world, and periods,
too, when I am just unavailable. . . . When I
"surface" again, I try to apply the poultices
and patch up the holes I've left in relationships
around me.*

—TONI CADE BAMBARA

We all need the space, from time to time, to do
whatever it is we need to do—write, practice, think,
dream, strategize. Sometimes we're physically there
but mentally preoccupied. Our estrangement can be
tough on the people around us, whose needs and expectations do not change when ours do. Lovers become threatened; children feel abandoned.

It might help to let our loved ones know we'll
be back, that we need this time to concentrate on
something that is important to us—may we please
have their help? We are entitled to put up our DO
NOT DISTURB signs; at the same time, we must learn
to respect that others need their space, too.

*On this day, I will seize space as I need it and give
others their space as they need it.*

January 19

BEAUTY

*When I found I had crossed dat line, I looked
at my hands to see if I was de same pusson.
There was such a glory ober ebery ting; de sun
came like gold through de trees, and ober de
fields, and I felt like I was in Heaben.*

—HARRIET TUBMAN

We have probably all experienced a similar feeling.
A child who has scored an A on a test may step out
of school and take note of the sun's wonderful
warmth and the delicious breeze. Finding ourselves
in love, we begin to notice the splendor around us—
in the trees, the flowers, and the sky. We are in a
state of hypersensitivity, attuned to the beauty we
normally take for granted.

There is glory around us always. Let us learn
to appreciate it more so we can start taking better
care of our environment. We nurture our souls when
we nurture our world.

*On this day, I will take five minutes to remember a
time when I felt exhilarated about something or
someone beautiful.*

January 20

MISTAKES

Every man got a right to his own mistakes.
Ain't no man that ain't made any.

—JOE LOUIS

None of us can expect to be infallible, yet we are often incensed when our parents, mates, or friends make mistakes. Perhaps we castigate them or gloat. Perhaps we hold them responsible for the rest of their lives. When we constantly harp on age-old mistreatments or goofs, we are trying to punish them; perhaps it's our anger we need to acknowledge and let go.

On this day, I pledge to take five minutes to see if there is some hurt I can let go.

SELF-IMAGE

I was always told I was the ugliest. That I was the dumbest. I was the blackest. That I would never be anything. My sister was much lighter than me, thin lips. I got the thick lips, the orange hair. I got all the beatings.

—BERTHA GILKEY

We have at times taken the hate and abuse that was inflicted upon us and turned it against ourselves. Some of us will take our anger and frustration out on our children, diminishing their self-esteem, reducing them, lest they feel too confident, too free, too happy. We turn against friends and family alike, fervid in our desire to cut them down to the size that suits us. At the receiving end of abuse, we wither under the onslaught.

It is time to examine ourselves. Have bitterness and envy enslaved us? Are we basket cases of poisonous emotions? Even if others may not know how to love us, we can learn to love ourselves.

On this day, I will take five minutes to note some of my good qualities. I will write these down and glance at my note throughout the day.

VISION

I have the original vision, and I see the film in its finished form before one frame is shot. When you get people dickering with your stuff, it distorts the vision.

—SPIKE LEE

Not only artists have their vision. We all have a vision of our lives, which encompasses our dreams and gives us the picture of fulfillment. When we permit others to dicker with our vision, the distorted result can cease to inspire and motivate us. Perhaps we aspire to become the scientist who develops a cure for sickle-cell anemia; if we succumb to our parents' exhortations to be a lawyer instead, we are bound to become resentful and fall short of our duties. We have cheated ourselves of our dreams.

Let's not allow others to reduce the scope of our vision.

On this day, I will take five minutes to think about my vision of my life, and make at least one concrete gesture toward making that vision a reality.

January 23

AGING/WISDOM

*The man who views the world at fifty the same
as he did at twenty has wasted thirty years of
his life.*

—MUHAMMAD ALI

Living means growing. As youngsters, we have limited life experience. Our parents put the roof over our head and food on the table. Our responsibilities are few.

As we age, we see more of life and experience more. We have victories and defeats, moments of great happiness and satisfaction, along with rejection and disappointment.

With all this occurring in our lives, we discover a lot about ourselves—and our capacity to love and nurture. We gain keener insight into ourselves and others, and become well versed in the fickleness and harshness and beauty of life.

*On this day, I will take five minutes to reflect on how
I viewed the world last year, two years ago, five years
ago, ten years ago. I will note how my attitudes have
changed.*

January 24

DISCOURAGEMENT

Many times during auditions, I was told that I couldn't carry a note with a bucket, and that I sure couldn't play the piano.

—RAY CHARLES

Discouragement can come from many sources. Friends, family, and strangers alike may savage our goals, our sense of self-worth. But no one outside ourselves is truly intimate with what is on the inside. No one knows the extent of our will, the urgency of our desire, or our perseverance.

Only we know what we are capable of, so we must guard that knowledge well against the "seek and destroy" missions of others. Some of us may find it simple to deny discouragement outright. Others will opt for more oblique ways to keep it from wreaking devastation—say through visualization or positive thinking. Whatever works.

We may grow weary from the fight or get bruised by our setbacks, but no one else can make us give up.

On this day, I will occasionally repeat silently to myself: "I am efficient and creative."

EQUALITY AT WORK

Equals make the best friends.
—AESOP, *from "The Two Pots"*

◼▮▮▮◼▮▮▮◼

Equality is a word that has long been a part of our history. Despite our political gains, we still strive for it today. While we may constantly remind ourselves of our value, it seems we're still trying to prove our worthiness in the workplace.

Well, nothing guarantees friendship. But certainly, if we can stand tall, without the bearing of the supplicant or beggar, we'll be better friends to ourselves if to no one else. And if our new standing enhances our lives both professionally *and* personally, then *equality* will have finally lived up to its reputation.

On this day, I will take five minutes of relaxation time and visualize myself as the equal of the highest-ranking member at my job. I will see myself as an equal participant in meetings and as devising strategies with this person as an equal.

MONEY

*America is a capitalist country,
and I am a capitalist.*

—ALONZO HERNDON

While some of our people may decry the system of economics under which so many of us suffer, many African-Americans have found rewards in capitalism.

Born enslaved, Alonzo Herndon ventured into several different businesses after the Civil War and met with his first big success when he opened a glamorous barbershop in Atlanta. He reinvested his profits in real estate and became a millionaire, then acquired a black insurance company that was about to go bankrupt. That small business grew into the second-largest black-owned insurance company in our country today. At the same time, Herndon put fellow African-Americans to work and insured others so they could begin their own businesses.

We can spend our days shaking our fingers at capitalism, or we can make it work for us.

On this day, I pledge to make a purchase at a black-owned establishment.

FAITH

Anticipate the good so that you may enjoy it.
—*ETHIOPIAN proverb*

Years ago, I left a reporter's job to accept a position as an editor at a new magazine. A few months later, the magazine folded and I landed back in my old position at my lower salary. As it turned out, my experience as an editor eventually helped propel me into an even more satisfying position at a prestigious publication. Had my temporary disappointment convinced me that life held nothing good for me, I doubt I would have had the energy or confidence to apply for the job I now hold.

Let's be sure to acknowledge the good. It is there and offers us opportunities and hope.

On this day, I will take five minutes to visualize in detail my future—which will be full of hope, luck, and opportunity.

January 28

JUDGING CHARACTER

You shake man han', you no shake him heart.
—BAHAMIAN proverb

It's always a bit sad when we have to warn our children, and each other, not to be so trusting of others. It makes the world sound frightening and dangerous. There is no joy in always having to be on our guard. A degree of wariness can be wise, but automatic suspicion of everyone can turn us into loners focused only on the evil that lurks "out there."

Let's simply be cautious in our dealings with others, trust our intuition if it seems to be generally on target, and accept that a handshake is an act of civility and not love. At the same time we need not erect impenetrable walls around ourselves, or suspect every smile. Mercifully, there is sincerity and friendship and romance in the world that can be ours if we are receptive to it.

I trust my judgment in gauging people, and will take relationships one step at a time. I will allow my intuition about people to work, knowing that the good or ill of those around me will be revealed.

January 29

AGGRESSIVENESS

*God gives nothing to those who keep their
arms crossed.*

—*AFRICAN proverb*

Seldom do wonderful things just drop into our laps.
Not only do we have to work for them, we have to
seize them for ourselves.

We need to make our desires for advancement
known at the proper time and through the proper
channels. It's okay if there's no immediate promotion. We need to listen to what they're telling us and
assess the situation. Perhaps there's more we can do
to put ourselves in line for the job we desire. After
a time, we can find the right opportunity to strike
again. Making things happen for ourselves is a
worthwhile habit to get into. When seeking romance,
for example, we're not going to meet the person of
our dreams just by sitting in our living rooms.

Let's free our arms to grab our dreams.

*On this day, I will make some small but concrete
gesture toward accomplishing one of my goals.*

COPING

Yeah, life hurts like hell, but this is how I keep going. I have a sense of humor, I've got my brothers and sisters. I've got the ability to make something out of nothing. I can clap my hands and make magic.

—BILL T. JONES

We all need to find the way to clap our hands and make magic.

Not one of us doesn't have burdens to bear, or sorrows, disappointments, and frustrations. If we let those define our lives, then, yes, we're going to focus on the hurt, and nothing will alleviate our suffering, nothing will give us joy.

Where do we find the joy? In whatever ignites our passions and gives us pleasure. For Bill Jones, joy comes from dancing, from his friends, from his sense of humor. For us, it might be from our gardens, our children, the poems we write, the quilts we stitch, the songs we sing, the time we spend in church or at the piano. We must actively look inside ourselves for fulfillment and be willing to experiment and stretch ourselves. This is how we all make magic.

On this day, I will take five minutes to think about what gives me joy and pleasure.

AFFIRMATIVE ACTION

I'm not a threatening black person to them. . . .
That's probably why I got hired. . . . But I also
got hired because I'm good. I have all the tools.
—BRANFORD MARSALIS

It can happen, in our careers, that someone will come along and assume we are there because of affirmative action and that we are not really up to the job. Someone else will come along and assume we are there because we're an Uncle Tom, an affable sort with no self-pride. Neither viewpoint represents the truth, and neither matters one whit.

We are in the job because we can handle it. We're good at what we do. We have the tools.

Unfortunately, throughout life, we must suffer the foolishness and ignorance of others. These attitudes may anger us, but we cannot afford to focus on them or they can eventually begin to stir up self-doubts. If we are always contemplating the perceptions of ourselves by others, and making the called-for adjustments, we'll waste our lives away.

On this day, I will focus on the job before me and do
it to the best of my ability.

SHYNESS

*I don't like making entrances unless I'm in
costume, at eight o'clock, on stage.*

— LEONTYNE PRICE

Of course, opera diva Leontyne Price probably
makes an "entrance" without even intending to, so
awesome is her talent and so regal her carriage. Yet
her manner is said to stem from a shyness of sorts.

Perhaps we've thought of ourselves as shy from
time to time, or done battle with that idea of ourselves. Shyness needn't cripple us as long as self-
confidence and industriousness exist. When we're
secure in our abilities and willing to put them "out
there," we'll come to terms with our self-
consciousness. Let's refrain from reinforcing the
"shy" self-image and using it as an excuse not to
realize our dreams.

*On this day, I will remember that I am creative and
capable of any task I put my mind to, and I will
remember that I have the power to project that
confidence whenever I want.*

February 2

TIME

We kill time; time buries us.
—JOAQUIM MARIA MACHADO DE ASSIS

How often do we find ourselves "killing time"? Probably more often than we'd like to admit.

Not that every minute must see you in a sweat, pursuing your goals. Everyone needs some quiet restorative "time-outs," particularly in today's noisy, stressful environment. This is "healing" time, which replenishes the soul. Overstressed, we can be rendered ineffective, even paralyzed.

The danger is in letting too many time-outs pile up. When that happens, it takes longer to get back on track; we have to work harder to make up for lost time, and events can defeat us if we are not careful. In this sense, time buries us.

We can guard against time-wasting by *making* time. This means allocating it properly—time to read, to exercise, to work toward our career goals, to spend with our families—and by *taking* time to assess our daily lives.

On this day, I will allocate time to do one thing that I haven't had time to do over the past four months.

February 3

DISCOURAGEMENT

We must not become discouraged.
—BOOKER T. WASHINGTON

When injustice and bigotry are still facts of our lives—when they now are parts of our children's lives—how can we help but become discouraged? Certainly we have to admit that there are disappointments in life—more, no doubt, than we'd planned on. There are career frustrations, unfulfilling marriages, wayward children, financial insecurity, and disease. Life can seem one long struggle with only the promise of death at the end.

Why not accept our moments of discouragement as part of life? Accept them, but then sweep them out, because we cannot afford to have discouragement linger. We can, instead, use our times of discouragement to reflect on our challenges—and then make a battle plan.

On this day, I will remember a time I felt discouraged or defeated. And then I will visualize myself taking control of the situation and succeeding.

UNITY

Sticks in a bundle are unbreakable.

—KENYAN (BONDEI) proverb

Sticks in a bundle symbolize unity, or Umoja, one of the seven principles we celebrate at Kwanzaa. As African-Americans, it is clear we must help ourselves. We must make alliances among ourselves, and stop the bickering, envy, and posturing that divide us. When we help other African-Americans, they can, in turn, help us or our children later. We can spend our money at African-American–owned stores, or buy products made by African-American–owned companies. Obviously, the more of us who make progress, the better for all of us.

Together, we are stronger. Apart, as strong as one alone might be, we cannot always stand up to the forces that work against us. One stick blows away in the wind. Bound to others, it stays in place.

Our potential for power is great—and power is a terrible thing to waste.

On this day, I pledge to buy at least one item from a black vendor or make a lunch date with an African-American colleague.

February 5

STRENGTH

One thing they cannot prohibit—
The strong men . . . coming on
The strong men gittin' stronger.
Strong men . . .
Stronger . . .

—STERLING BROWN

We get stronger when we demand a better education for our children, when we search out the teachers who care. We get stronger when we demand safety and security in our neighborhoods. We get stronger when we learn about our heritage, and pass it on to our children. We get stronger when we stand up and shout "No!" to discrimination and abuse. We get stronger when we value our bodies and minds, and nurture them accordingly. We get stronger when we dream, stronger still when we pursue our dreams. We get stronger day by day, stronger when we succeed, stronger when we fail—because failure cannot diminish our strength but can add to it. We get stronger when we are willing to do what is necessary.

On this day, I will do at least one concrete thing that gets me closer to my goal.

STEREOTYPES

*One of the sad commentaries on the way
women are viewed in our society is that we have
to fit one category. I have never felt that I had
to be in one category.*

—FAYE WATTLETON

Categories can never reflect who we really are. We
make a serious mistake when we attempt to define a
person by one aspect of his or her being. Labels—
such as Republican, Democrat, feminist, recovering
alcoholic, husband, mother, lawyer, Catholic, welfare
recipient—can become loaded with fallacious impli-
cations about our values, worth, or motivations.
Let's acknowledge that the soul and humanity of an
individual are not to be captured and defined in a
label or category.

*On this day, I will reflect upon one of the following: a
woman I know; a man I know; a person of the same
race or religion whom I know; a person of a different
race or religion whom I know. Then I will take five
minutes to note qualities that are unique to him or
her or different from the stereotypical image of that
kind of person.*

LONELINESS

There was no loneliness in the living room. So it was a good part, and maybe the best part, of the house.

—JUNE JORDAN

We need people in our lives because we are nourished and enriched by their presence. We need the laughter, the conversation, the debate, and the communion. While some may challenge such a notion, preferring solitude, it may be because they do not wish to involve themselves with the needs and wants of others, or they do not wish to expend the effort.

Still, it is possible to feel lonely when surrounded by friends and family. Ultimately, we are all lone souls in the universe; hence our drive to find partnership with God or a Higher Power.

Loneliness can hurt, can make us ache and despair. We need to find ways to quench the longing; when we spend time in the living room of life, our despair is lifted and our emotions are permitted engagement and release.

On this day, I pledge to try to be sensitive to the loneliness of others, and to make an effort to reach out to them.

February 8

FREEDOM

*We have dared to be free; let us dare to be so
by ourselves and for ourselves.*
—JEAN-JACQUES DESSALINES, *Proclamation,
January 1, 1804*

Freedom wasn't won easily. It took years of struggle.
African-American casualties were high.

Now that freedom is ours, we have to ask ourselves, is it really? What others expect from us has the power to shackle us—if we allow it to.

At Kwanzaa, we celebrate Kujichagulia, the principle of self-determination whereby we define ourselves. Every individual has this duty. If we don't take it seriously, we are in danger of relinquishing our power to others—to all the parents, mates, friends, and enemies who want to put us in "our place" and tell us who we are and what we can or can't do. It takes effort and vigilance to be free. It's worth it.

On this day, I will take five minutes to remember a time when I had a choice to make. I will visualize myself making the right choice.

February 9

GENEROSITY

Before you marry keep both eyes open;
after marriage shut one.

—*JAMAICAN proverb*

In the process of falling in love, we are often so taken by a person's good points that we fail to see his, shall we say, negative quirks. Even if we do recognize that he doesn't wash dishes or pick up his dirty underwear, we probably focus on the way he massages our shoulders or whips up spectacular French toast. Once we've been married awhile, however, we may conclude that we would rather have clean dishes and laundry *in* the hamper than relaxed shoulders and brunch.

But in any long-term relationship, we need to remember all the wonderful things that brought us together with our loved one. If that means closing *both* eyes—it's time to do some serious thinking. But if it means closing one, well, that ain't half bad.

On this day, I will be more generous and accepting
with the people who are important in my life.

February 10

ADAPTABILITY

What most successful blacks learn is that most everything can, in fact, be learned—how to talk, how to dress, how to groom an image for success. The important thing is to recognize what is not known—and then learn it.
—AUDREY EDWARDS and CRAIG K. POLITE, *from* Children of the Dream

When we enter any new work environment, it feels foreign to us until we've been there awhile and have developed a feel for it. We can learn what works there by asking and by observing.

There may be some who "get away with" more than others, but everyone, black and white, tends to conform to a general set of norms that applies to a particular office. As African-Americans we need not always fear that we are selling our souls in the workplace just because we *choose* to conform.

On this day, I will spend five minutes thinking about what it takes to make a cozy fit in my workplace, or the place where I might want to work. I won't be afraid to make changes to fit in. But I will not compromise myself.

February 11

FORETHOUGHT

Look before you leap.
—AESOP, *from "The Fox and the Goats"*

✖▐▌▌▌▌✖▐▌▌▌▌✖

We've all had our impetuous moments—usually they're the ones we shake our heads over. Yet spontaneity should have a place in our lives or life will become so dull and preplanned we might as well stay in bed.

We often blame our mistakes on impetuousness. So why don't we credit it for some of the good stuff in our lives?

There are times we've just got to say, "Now, wait a minute. Let me think about this." That's all. It doesn't mean we've got to say no. (Some of us know we have trouble saying that little word and so we overcompensate.) It doesn't imply we're not decisive, quick-witted individuals. Looking, thinking, "sleeping on it" before leaping just means we're in control.

On this day, I will take five minutes of relaxation time to visualize a situation in the past in which I made an impetuous decision—but in my visualization, I will act with serenity and deliberation.

February 12

PEACE

*I hope never to be at peace. I hope to make my
life manageable, and I think it's fairly
manageable now. But, oh, I would never accept
peace. That seems death.*

—JAMAICA KINCAID

In our African-American community, can there ever
be peace for one when there is such degradation and
despair for so many? Can we afford to be complacent
when our people are struggling?

There will always be personal goals and communal goals that have not been met, and no peace
until we reach them. Perhaps we need to rethink
peace as something that can be quaffed from time to
time for nourishment and refreshment, not as a liq-
uor to down all at once to bring on inebriation. That
kind of stupor can indeed be death.

*On this day, I will do one concrete thing that furthers
me toward one of my goals.*

February 13

LOVE

Love without esteem cannot go far or reach high. It is an angel with only one wing.

—ALEXANDRE DUMAS, FILS

We might even ask if love is *possible* without esteem. Or is something else at work—pity, lust, loneliness, fear, neediness? When there is mutual respect between partners, there is the unvoiced acknowledgment that we are growing, changing individuals. Our love accepts and encourages that growth, even if we must struggle against feeling nervous or threatened.

In love, we learn how to respect the needs and dreams of our mate. We offer encouragement and support, not ridicule and cynicism. But it is also vital that we hold ourselves in high esteem, that we do not "lose ourselves" in making the relationship work. When we respect ourselves—our needs and dreams —our partner will respect us, too.

On this day, I will make a small gesture of support to the special person in my life.

SELF-HELP

*"Self-help" isn't enough in a milieu of
institutionalized racism.*

—CARL T. ROWAN

First, let's understand the idea behind "self-help." It
doesn't mean we need to eschew government resources to help ourselves. Yes, it is important to do
all we can do on our own, but it's also necessary for
us to lobby the government for jobs and programs
that will benefit us. The government helps people all
the time, from corporations to foreign countries.

Let's not be bulldozed by those who say we ask
for too much. We pay taxes, and either we or our
forebears have sacrificed for this country. We have
gained or maintained freedom for others by going to
war. We have improved this country through the civil
rights movement.

Once we demand the things we need to help
ourselves, we need to use those resources wisely. Let's
realize that self-help means mining *all* the opportunities we have available.

*On this day, I will pledge to seize and create
opportunities for a better future for our community
and country.*

MAKING DEALS

Women don't get hung up, making deals the way men do.

—SHIRLEY CHISHOLM

In a sense, we all make deals. With our families, our lovers, and especially ourselves. The trick is in knowing which deals are to our ultimate benefit, and which will weaken us.

I know a woman who was mocked by another for helping her husband make some career progress. The second woman announced, "I could never put the needs of another in front of my own!"

The first woman's goal in supporting her husband's work was to help him earn the money to buy a house for their family and to get to a point of financial stability so she could dedicate her energy to her own dreams. And she did.

Let's not let shortsightedness dissuade us from deals that can ultimately benefit us.

On this day, I will take five minutes to remember a time I made a deal that made me stronger, wealthier, happier or gave me more hope.

February 16

POSITIVE THINKING

*To be a great champion you must believe you
are the best. If you're not, pretend you are.*
—MUHAMMAD ALI

Pretending we are successful at what we do conditions us for becoming successful. When we adopt the
mind-set of the champion, and follow through with
action, we are well on our way.

Years ago, a friend of mine lost a noticeable
amount of weight and looked great. When I asked
how he did it, he replied, "I think thin." By acting
like a thin person, he ate more judiciously and began
to exercise. He shed the pounds and remains trim
today.

Acting the part can persuade you, in time, that
you *are* the part, even before you really are. We all
fail once in a while; it's part of life, which is not
always within our control. When we see ourselves as
winners, though, we accept our failures and move on.

*On this day, I will take five minutes and visualize
that I have what I want to have or am what I want
to be.*

CONFUSION

A man is sometimes lost in the dust of his own raising.

—*DAVID RUGGLES*

Sometimes we lose track of ourselves. We rush to work, do our jobs, rush home, feed and bathe the children, clean the house, then fall exhausted into bed. Then we wake up and do it all over again.

These things need to be done, of course. Bills have got to be paid and children don't raise themselves. But we all need a little quiet time, a time to let the dust settle, when we can take stock of our lives, our feelings, and our goals. Time spent in front of the television doesn't count. We must make it a point to nurture ourselves and refuel our spirits. We can take a warm bath, find a peaceful spot in the park, sit in our beds with some soothing music on in the background—the idea is not to focus on tasks but on our thoughts.

When we take time out this way, life doesn't get away from us but can be lived more productively, with control and composure.

On this day, I will take five minutes and reassess what I am doing with my life, where I want to go, and what I want to accomplish.

MONEY

Let the Afro-American depend on no party, but on himself for his salvation. Let him to continue to education, to character, and above all, to put money in his purse. When he has money, and plenty of it, parties and races will become his servants.

—IDA B. WELLS

Many of us have grown up with the notion that money is the root of all evil. We are conditioned to believe that an individual with money has sold his soul. Yet, out in the world, it is obvious that money buys us comfort, choices, and peace of mind. It can be difficult to reconcile the two extremes, to find that middle ground where we can function without guilt.

We do indeed need to have money in our bank accounts. It allows us to live without desperation, and thereby frees us from a subservient position. Let us use our money wisely, refrain from spending it as if there were no tomorrow, and learn how to make our money work for us.

On this day, I pledge to put a fixed amount of my paycheck, no matter how small, into a savings account every week.

February 19

PRIDE

*You can't just fight for the money because if
you do, after the first round you can think you
don't need to take all the punishment.
. . . You fight for the belt plus the pride.*

—EVANDER HOLYFIELD

When we are able to take home from our jobs a sense
of pride and honor, the money becomes secondary.
The "punishment"—office politics, frustrations with
the boss, long hours and unappreciated effort—becomes bearable. The challenge, then, is to find work
that we enjoy doing. And while we may not all be
able to make an immediate career switch, we can ask
ourselves why we're working. If our ultimate goal is
simply to afford our children more possibilities, then
that is where we derive our honor and pride. Even if
no one confers on us a title or belt, we are champions
nonetheless.

*On this day, I will do at least one thing that will
advance me toward one of my goals.*

February 20

QUIET

I love to walk on the Sabbath, for all is so
peaceful, the noise and labor of everyday life
has ceased; and in perfect silence we can
commune with nature and with Nature's God.
—CHARLOTTE L. FORTEN

We seem to fill up our lives with noise. Even in solitude, outside noise presses in on us—street sounds, neighbors, the hubbub of our own family. Some of us may be in the habit of flipping on a radio or television when we enter our homes, as if we're afraid of being alone with ourselves. Do we fear what we might think, or feel?

In silence we are able to shake off some of the stress that keeps us from functioning at full power. In silence, our spirits are healed. Our thoughts are free to roam, to create, to solve, to muse. In serene outdoor spots, we absorb more intensely the beauty and wonder of nature.

Let's not deny ourselves the power of silence.

On this day, I will take five minutes to be in total
silence and passively observe and note the images that
float before my mind's eye.

February 21

ROLE MODELS

I could see that my significance as an individual
was small. . . . I had become, whether I liked it
or not, a symbol, representing my people. . . .
I could not run away from this situation.

—MARIAN ANDERSON

As we achieve, we become role models for others. People look to us for inspiration, asking how we did it, hungry for advice on how they, too, can reach their goals.

While we are first responsible to ourselves to lead sober, sane, and healthy lives, it is obvious how important our doing so is to our people. African-Americans are plagued by negative stereotypes. By being industrious, committed, concerned and creative, we define ourselves in positive terms.

We need not be opera divas to represent our people. We can be hardworking nurses, teachers, shopkeepers, or parents and affect the lives of those who know us. All of our achievements have merit.

On this day, I will pledge to do my job to the best of
my ability—and to be a role model for those around me.

February 22

CONFLICT

*I glory in conflict, that I may hereafter exult
in victory.*

—FREDERICK DOUGLASS

Although many would wish it otherwise, there is simply no escaping conflict. It is fundamental to human life. We experience it early, as infants, when we want our bottle or toy or some sharp implement, but mother takes it away. We experience conflict at home, at school, in the playground. As adults, we experience it with our friends and loved ones, at work, on the bus, anywhere.

African-Americans are no strangers to conflict. Our history is rife with heroes and heroines who did not shrink back from the bitter and often brutal realities of conflict. It is certain we would have made no progress by avoiding it.

While we need not go out of our way to look for conflict—and some enjoy a good fight as much as a good meal—we can accept its inevitability and find our individual style for dealing with it.

*On this day, I will take five minutes to remember a
time when I was in a challenging situation and
triumphed.*

RESEARCH

May God preserve us from "If I had known"!
—HAUSA proverb

▰▰▰▰▰▰

How often have we heard people moan, "If I had known he was a such-and-such, I never would have married him." Or "If I had known it was going to be so much work, I never would have done it."

Well, we didn't know and it's really pretty futile to sit around wishing we had. But what we can get out of such an experience is the knowledge that we probably need to get more information in the future. Perhaps we need to spend more time with people before making commitments. Perhaps we need to gather more background on projects before we embark on them.

Let's look at information as a means to make the right decisions. It can save us a lot of time, energy, and effort!

On this day, I will see if I have all the information I need to make a decision regarding a mate or to accomplish one of my goals. If not, I pledge to gather it.

February 24

SATISFACTION

I rewrite all the way to the printer.
I'm never satisfied.

—TONI MORRISON

Whatever our work—raising children, performing our job at the office—there is always room for improvement. Maybe we could take the kids to the library or museums more often, or dedicate more energy to our tasks at work. We generally sense it when we're functioning at only half speed.

Taking all this into account, there also comes a point when we must content ourselves with our efforts. If there remains a nagging sense that we could have/should have done more, let's use it to guide us in our future efforts.

Let's never be satisfied—but let's not let ourselves become paralyzed by perfectionism or regret.

On this day, I will take five minutes to remember a time when I felt very satisfied, and I will take that feeling and let it inspire me in my endeavors today.

HELPING OTHERS

A sure way for one to lift himself up is by helping to lift someone else.

—BOOKER T. WASHINGTON

Depression can be overwhelming. Try as we may, there are times when it seems all we can do is wallow in our own sorrowful mood, reflecting on how bleak and unsatisfying life appears.

Shifting the focus to someone else's condition can be our best means of *self*-help. Volunteering at a nursing home or Big Brother/Sister program, cuddling abandoned babies at the hospital, spending a few hours at a homeless shelter or delivering meals to homebound people with AIDS can make us feel better about ourselves as we simultaneously help those in need.

On this day, I will do something for a fellow African-American. Perhaps I will begin volunteering in the community or just send a pretty notecard to an elderly aunt living alone or take a bag of bakery cookies to a recently widowed neighbor. Whatever I choose, what I do today will be from the heart and with no expectation of return.

February 26

COLLECTIVE WORK
AND RESPONSIBILITY

*If farmers do not cultivate their fields, the
people in the town will die of hunger.*

—*GUINEAN proverb*

As the farmer cultivates his fields, we must cultivate
our lives. If we neither attend to the soil nor bother
to sow any seeds, there will be no harvest, no bounty
to sustain us or our children.

It is incumbent upon each and every one of us
to tend our lives with care, to put forth unceasing
effort. Whenever we succeed, the outcome benefits
us personally. And the African-American community also benefits because we are in a position to
"feed" others—to help them directly or to inspire by
our example.

*On this day, I will do at least one thing that
advances me toward one of my goals.*

February 27

CONTROL/DIRECTION

To me, Jesus was a phenomenal figure. . . . He was a revolutionary, but He knew how to conserve His energy.

—WESLEY SNIPES

Perhaps we need to learn how to say no more often. To others, but also to ourselves. We get the idea in our heads that we must do everything, try everything, be everything. We distract ourselves from our most important goals, but we can't figure out why we feel so dissatisfied. We feel remorse at the wasting of time, but we still don't have a clue as to how to concentrate our efforts.

Some temperaments thrive on constant activity, but if we feel our pace is not allowing us to accomplish what we want, we need to apportion our time and energy to serve us better.

On this day, I will take five minutes to reevaluate how I spend my time and energy.

February 28

DIPLOMACY

Maybe the worst somebody would ever say of me was: He was fairly undiplomatic in the way he tried to get things done. But at least he tried to get things done.

—BRYANT GUMBEL

Diplomacy is, indeed, an art. It can make a good boss into a great boss, a good parent into a great parent, a good friend/lover/spouse into a great one. Yet sometimes we can trip all over ourselves trying to be diplomatic. In wanting to spare others' feelings we may garble the message and end up confusing or even insulting the person we aim to spare.

There are instances when because of the time involved or the urgency of the situation, we need to speak our mind directly and without guilt. Also, when diplomacy is not used with us, it is not necessary to search for it ourselves.

We don't need to run around always trying to pick a fight. What we want is the clarity of mind to realize when straight talk is the best talk.

On this day, I will take five minutes to remember a time when I spoke honestly and directly to a person and benefited from my candor.

COURAGE

Courage may be the most important of all virtues, because without it one cannot practice any other virtue with consistency.

—MAYA ANGELOU

Without courage, we are bound to feel vulnerable. We cannot be generous because people will take advantage of us. We cannot be kind because people will think we're weak. We cannot be honest because people will use it against us. We cannot trust because we'll be stabbed in the back.

In summoning courage, we must first be willing to challenge our fear. Second, we must act in the face of it. And finally, we must have faith in the outcome. Each time we do this, we get a little stronger, a little braver.

I will take five minutes to remember a time when I felt courageous, and I will use that feeling to fuel me toward taking a step toward one of my goals today.

March 1

PURPOSE

I don't know the key to success, but the key to failure is trying to please everybody.

—BILL COSBY

<hr>

Our world is filled with critics—well-meaning (usually) parents, siblings, spouses, lovers, friends, co-workers, bosses, and mentors who think they can neatly pinpoint our deficits and prescribe appropriate treatment. They seem to know what we're doing wrong with our lives and have a good idea of what we ought to do. If we take them *all* to heart, we will probably get hundreds of varying suggestions.

Should we disregard them all? No, we might actually miss out on some worthwhile advice. It is possible to listen to others without becoming unduly influenced by them.

We need to stay true to ourselves, however, and this is crucial. It prevents us from being torn in a hundred different directions and losing ourselves in the process.

On this day, I will take five minutes to relax and focus on one of my goals. I will visualize attaining that goal without being unduly influenced by others.

March 2

SACRIFICE

Becoming a world-class figure skater meant long hours of practice while sometimes tolerating painful injuries. It meant being totally exhausted sometimes, and not being able to do all the things I wanted to do when I wanted to do them.

—DEBI THOMAS

No champion becomes one without discipline. Enjoying our work helps enormously, so let's commit ourselves to a path that gives us pleasure and fulfillment along the way. Identifying our talents and interests helps us in choosing the right route. When we love what we're doing, few sacrifices are too large.

On this day, I will take five minutes to remember some of the sacrifices I have made to accomplish one of my past goals, and I will also remember the rich feeling of satisfaction I had after attaining that goal.

March 3

FOCUSING

When I leave the ballpark, I leave everything there. When I hit the driveway, I become a husband and father.

—BO JACKSON

We've often heard it said we should not bring our romantic or family troubles into the office—"it's not professional." But there's no handy reverse warning about bringing our work problems home.

It's not the easiest thing to separate all our selves. Sometimes we walk in the door and are still working out that problem from the office or carrying negative emotions we can live without.

For our mate's sake, for our kids, for ourselves, we've got to learn how to shift. Because no matter whom we live with—our parents, wife and children, or friends—dumping a foul mood on them is wrong.

On this day, I will use common courtesy and focus on what I am doing at the moment.

INDIVIDUAL RESPONSIBILITY

It is impossible to raise and educate a race in the mass. All revolutions and improvements must start with individuals.

—JOHN W. E. BOWEN

We African-Americans have our leaders to speak for us, our organizations to work for us, and our clergy to pray for us—but unless we, each and every one of us, make the individual commitment to rise to our full potential, we cannot expect our community to do the same.

It pains us when we hear and read of the problems our people face. Despair grips us, and for some, hopelessness sets in. What can we do when the enormity of the situation makes us wonder whether we have the energy or wherewithal to fight it?

We can each pledge to do our personal best. At school and at work, in our homes and in all our relationships with each other. Doing this we set an example for our children, and gradually, but steadily, we uplift ourselves.

On this day, I will take one concrete action to further me in one of my goals.

March 5

PERSEVERANCE

I'm inspired when I walk down the street and still see people trying. A lot of them look as if they're on their last leg, but they're still getting up somehow.

—FAITH RINGGOLD

How dare we give up, break down, and roll over when so many who have it worse hang in there?! Yes, we do become discouraged, and no one can compare his tragedy or his secrets to ours. Perhaps our threshold for pain is lower than our neighbor's—what do we do?

We must always look for inspiration. Reading about others' travails and how they vanquished prejudice, poverty, ill health, and every kind of disability can restore our faith in the human spirit—particularly our own!

It's natural for our spiritual batteries to run low at times—no disgrace in that. But it's up to us to recharge them so that our will to fight, to persevere and win is strengthened.

On this day, I will think about a relative or some other person whose work and/or life inspires me.

FIRST STEPS

*I knew someone had to take the first step and
I made up my mind not to move.*

—ROSA PARKS

First steps are always scary. When we take a first step, we are ultimately acting alone. With a first step, we take a leap of faith that we will wind up on both feet when all the dust settles. All of us have some experience in taking first steps. When we initiate a move toward friendship, or make the attempt to apologize and patch up a relationship, it's possible we'll fail. Ditto when we start a new job or career, or commit to a romantic partner. While the risks may not be as frightening as those that Rosa Parks took, they are nonetheless significant and meaningful as they are our own intimate tests of character. With a first step, we challenge ourselves and our fears.

*On this day, I will take five minutes to remember a
time when I took a first step—started a project, made
up with a friend, introduced myself to a future loved
one—and I will feel the emotions and sweet
sensations of that initial move blossoming.*

EXCELLENCE

Strive to make something of yourselves;
then strive to make the most of yourselves.
—ALEXANDER CRUMMELL

Life is a struggle, and very often we tend to settle for less than our dreams. We do not realize our potential but stop far short of it. As a result, we hear the nagging voice inside ourselves, the guilty voice that tells us we have failed. It's a demoralizing force that makes us question our talents, our ability, our drive—in fact, our very worthiness as human beings.

Realize that it is never, *never* too late to go for your dreams. Our achievements at fifty-two are as precious as those at twenty-two, if not more precious. We need to appraise our unique abilities and determine how we can best put them to use.

On this day, I will spend five minutes remembering
something I did in the past that made me proud.
Then I will visualize how I could have done it better.

March 8

POWER

There does not have to be powerlessness.
The power is within ourselves.

—FAYE WATTLETON

When we surrender our personal power, we cede our rights, our progress, and our emotions to others. We can reverse the situation when we take back the reins of power over our lives. Awakening ourselves, involving ourselves, keeping ourselves energized and alert will help us focus on the things we need to do to make our lives fulfilling—and to make our community strong.

On this day, I will take five minutes to meditate on the power within me. I will feel it welling up inside me, and I will visualize myself using it in my everyday life.

March 9

PRIDE

*The only excuse for pride in individuals or races
is the fact of their own achievements.*

—FREDERICK DOUGLASS

It is not what we say that counts, but what we do.
What matters is not what we wear—our Malcolm X
caps and kente cloth garments—or the African art
that adorns our homes, but our accomplishments.

While the exterior expressions of cultural pride
have their function, they are practically meaningless
if not accompanied by action. "I'm black and I'm
proud" must be followed by "I make A's at school;
I excel at my profession; I can feed, clothe, and educate my children; I can care for my parents in their
advanced years." Whatever is appropriate for us at
this time in our lives.

Let "black is beautiful" extend to "black is active, black is productive, black is responsible." Then
we can indeed be proud.

*On this day, I will take five minutes to look at a
symbol of my pride in my heritage—my "X" cap, my
family photos, African cloth—and try to see it as just
that—a symbol to inspire me to greater excellence
throughout the day.*

March 10

EDUCATION

The masses must move, but it must be the classes that move them.

—WILLIAM SAUNDERS SCARBOROUGH

Educator William Saunders Scarborough had fun with a little wordplay here. For "classes" read education, and you will get the point: With education, we have mobility onward and upward.

Education gives us wings. It has the power to expand our lives and to inspire us. Without it, we cannot compete, and we play into the hands of those who'd be quite content to have us drop out of the competition.

There are teachers for all of us, caring people who entered the profession because they wanted to help. We must search them out. And after our formal education, we must continue to learn if we are to continue to grow.

On this day, I will read the front page of the newspaper, read a magazine, or read a chapter from a book, or I will offer my knowledge to someone who might benefit from it.

CHANGE

Every small, positive change we can make in ourselves repays us in confidence in the future.
—ALICE WALKER

In our habit of "thinking big," we often neglect the smaller things we can do to add value to our lives or aid us in accomplishing our goals. It might be that we'd like to improve our eating habits. We can make a start by including fresh fruit at our meals and for snacks. A small thing, but it can give us incentive to make other changes.

Our small changes have a greater chance for success because we pinpoint manageable tasks. We are therefore less likely to be defeated by the enormity of our goals or the hectic pace of our lives. Meeting one small goal at a time gives us the confidence to set more goals and foresee a bright future as we do so.

On this day, I pledge to do at least one small thing toward improving my life.

March 12

SUCCESS

In some sense, the black professional's problem is that each of us who succeeds in the white world feels we've succeeded at the expense of our brothers.

—KENNETH MCCLANE

While it's true that many of us feel we have succeeded at the expense of our brothers and sisters, in fact the opposite is true. When we succeed, we're in a position to look out for and help African-Americans. It is possible for the white powers-that-be to see that the sky doesn't fall when we succeed—and this can result in the hiring of other African-Americans.

So let's relieve ourselves of guilt, which may cloud our sense of achievement, but use our gains to benefit our brothers and sisters as well.

On this day, I will take five minutes to think about the ways my accomplishing one of my goals will help other African-Americans.

PRIVACY

Black people don't have any privacy.
                    —Anonymous, heard in Harlem

It's important for African-Americans—as it is for everyone—to question our leaders. The problem is, it's difficult for us to do so when even our black forums—our magazines, newspapers, radio and TV shows—are open to all.

This lack of privacy can put us between a rock and a hard place. Perhaps we agree with a conservative African-American, but we don't want to fuel white racists so we keep silent. Or perhaps we disagree, but we keep silent because we don't want whites to hear us arguing or focus on our "disunity."

We need to get together to talk among ourselves—with the goal of seeing what ideas are good or bad, viable or not viable, useful or not useful.

On this day, I will choose one likely person and begin the long process of forging an alliance based on trust with him or her, so that we might have a candid exchange of ideas.

                                        March 14

EXPERIMENTATION

*People have to have permission to write, and
they have to be given the space to breathe and
stumble. They have to be given time to develop
and to reveal what they can do.*

—TONI CADE BAMBARA

Most of us are eager to determine our own political,
philosophical, and temperamental style—to define
who we are, what we believe, how we think and react
to things. In order to find this personal style, we may
end up trying on a lot of different attitudes, poses,
and philosophies like so many different hats.

It's okay to explore and experiment, to try on
different ideas to see what fits most comfortably. It
takes time for people to develop, to see what they
have to contribute and find what suits them. Life
does not force us to wear one hat all our lives; we
have permission to try new ones all the time.

*On this day, I will take five minutes to remember the
different changes I have gone through up to this point
in my life. I will acknowledge that it is okay to
change and that there is nothing wrong with going
through different phases.*

March 15

OPTIMISM

*What seems to be a great loss or punishment
often turns out to be a blessing. I know,
through my own experience, that God never
closes one door without opening another.*
—YOLANDE D. HERRON

It is difficult, in our times of profound disappointment, to look for the silver lining. When someone close to us dies, we are allowed to grieve and friends rally around us. But when we have fallen out with a friend, broken off with a lover, or been fired, people can be less patient with us.

When we harbor feelings of failure and self-pity, we can turn away people and opportunities without realizing it. We need to acknowledge that our failures, rejections, and disappointments do not reflect upon our value as people. When we are suddenly forced to examine our lives, we often stumble upon insights we might not have gained had our misfortune not occurred.

*On this day I will take five minutes to consider a
time I was disappointed but went on to find
satisfaction and succeeded. I will use that memory to
inspire me today.*

DEPENDENCY

*The greatest thing I ever was able to do was
give a welfare check back. I brought it back
. . . and said, "Here. I don't need this
anymore."*

—WHOOPI GOLDBERG

Accepting help does not mean we are forever dependent. Dependency can be a frightening thing,
since it is a condition that can rob us of control and
sap our self-esteem. Maintaining a belief in ourselves
can be dicey when we are forced to ask for help. The
longer we are indebted to someone else, the harder
it becomes to shake our habit.

While there is no shame in asking for help,
we've got to be able to say at some point, "No, thank
you."

*On this day, I pledge to sit down to consider what I
owe, whether the debt is financial or a debt I may owe
a person who has helped me emotionally. I also
pledge, if the debt is financial, to repay more than the
minimum payment this month, and if it is emotional,
to make some small gesture of thanks to the person.*

ANGER

When you clench your fist, no one can put anything in your hand, nor can your hand pick up anything.

—*ALEX HALEY, from* Roots

When we live with anger and hatred, we close ourselves to life's possibilities. We learn to see only the negatives—the evil, brutality, selfishness, and destructiveness. We become blind to the kindness people try to offer us, and we deny that we can find anything genuinely good or worthwhile in life. If we are fortunate enough to get close to another person, our intimacy may eventually erode with our constant suspicion, distrust, ill temper, or pessimism.

It is unlikely that our clenched fist will spontaneously relax and open. We may first have to notice that it *is* clenched before we can gradually begin to loosen it. We may have to practice trusting people, and learn how to pull back when we find ourselves relapsing into our old negative habits.

At the end of this day, I will take five minutes to remember at least one good thing that happened to me, or a task, however small, that I completed that gave me satisfaction.

PERSEVERANCE

By trying often, the monkey learns to jump from the tree.

—CAMEROON *proverb*

The monkey does not conclude, after his first awkward landing, "I was not meant to jump, or to climb." Perseverance gets him back up the tree.

When we look at successful people, we get the impression that they have known *only* success. But success stories are full of tales of rejection slips and bankruptcies and years of unrecognized work and thwarted ambition. We've heard the "overnight sensations" tell us how they toiled for years at their craft, waiting tables or working temp jobs until they finally met with success.

Look at baseball. Batting .300 is considered good, and that's only getting a hit one time out of every three at bat!

On this day, I will do at least one thing that will advance me toward one of my goals.

March 19

PREJUDICE

*Terms like "prejudice" and "racism" often miss
the full scope of racial devaluation in our society,
implying as they do that racial devaluation
comes primarily from the strongly prejudiced,
not from "good people."*

—CLAUDE M. STEELE

There are a number of good people out there who do
not hate us but are merely uninformed or mis-
informed.

Some of us may want to take it upon ourselves
to educate these people. Yet we get so tired of ex-
plaining our frustrations and defending our positions
on all the issues all the time.

We really have no viable choice but to be our
own best friend, and a best friend to other African-
Americans—showing one another encouragement,
appreciating one another's natural talents, and supporting one another however we can.

*On this day, I will make a special point of telling an
African-American that I have confidence in her
abilities and expect that she will succeed in anything
she desires and puts her mind to.*

March 20

ETERNITY

It is only what is written upon the soul of man
that will survive the wreck of time.

—*FRANCIS GRIMKÉ*

There is nothing wrong with wanting to live comfortable lives, to provide the best for our families and give our children more options than we had. Yes, money helps. It smooths the way and allows us to live with far fewer worries and stresses.

But ask this: When we die, how will they pay tribute to us? Will they say we bought a new car every year, that we consumed no wine under fifty dollars a bottle? Hardly. They will tabulate our kindness and contributions, praise our generosity and our concern and consideration for others. It is, after all, what is in our souls—not our checkbooks—that people remember.

On this day, I will take five minutes to write down
five positive character traits in myself—traits that
have nothing to do with the distribution of money or
generosity with material things.

SELF-RELIANCE

Everyone is more or less the master of his own fate.
—AESOP, from "The Traveler and Fortune"

We can all make choices. While we can't pick our parents, there are many things we *can* control. We can study in the library if not at home, apply for a scholarship, complete our education, select our careers, change our careers, choose our friends, determine how we spend our time—productively or not. Instead of spending the evening in front of the television, we can go for a walk, do yoga, read a book or newspaper, update our résumé, listen to music that nurtures us, cook up a pot of healthful soup to freeze, or write a letter. It's when we take charge of our hours on this earth that we are truly the masters of our fate.

On this day, I will look at something I would like to spend more time doing—then I will devise a way to spend more time doing it.

March 22

EMOTIONS

*Our feelings are our most genuine paths to
knowledge. They are chaotic, sometimes painful,
sometimes contradictory, but they come from
deep within us. And we must key into those
feelings.... This is how new visions begin.*

—AUDRE LORDE

We sometimes think we must quash our negative
feelings, that nothing productive can come from
them. But worry can move us to find a creative solution, envy can drive us to apply ourselves more,
and even panic can make us look around for an alternative. The trick is in not getting locked into any
one position, not getting scared stiff so that we cannot do anything to help ourselves.

Let's be ready to legitimize and examine our
feelings. Out of them we can harvest deeper insights,
potential opportunities and new visions for our lives.

*On this day, I pledge to acknowledge all my emotions
and find ways to make them work for me in a
positive way.*

March 23

FEAR

You got people out there with this scar on their brains, and they will carry that scar to their graves. The mark of fear is not easily removed.
—ERNEST J. GAINES, *from*
The Autobiography of Miss Jane Pittman

We all have fears—large and small, serious and trivial. Some fears handicap us more than others; those fears may be the harder ones to deal with.

People talk about "a healthy sense of fear." When fear makes us cautious in an unfamiliar or crime-prone neighborhood, fear works for us. But a fear that paralyzes us, such as fear of failure (or success), prevents us from living our lives as fully as we should.

We do not need to settle for a life plagued by fear. It may take time, but we can rid ourselves of fears if we are committed to doing so.

On this day, I will spend five minutes examining any fears I might have about accomplishing my goals. Then I will visualize myself addressing and breaking free of those fears.

March 24

TRUST

I am not afraid to trust my sisters—not I.
—ANGELINA GRIMKÉ

━━━▰▰▰▰━━━

So often we look at our sisters, or brothers, with suspicion. We guard our territory well, and are leery of those who might try to usurp it. At work we become competitors, hung up by the belief that only one of us can make it, so we'll do what's necessary to make sure we are that one. In love, too, we are competitors, and so we learn to belittle our rivals and anticipate their every action as a move to do us in.

Trust is hard-earned, we've heard. Some counsel us to trust no one. It may seem like the smartest way to run our lives, thinking the worst of others and never letting down our guard.

If we can't learn to trust each other, we are doomed. In trusting, we can help others, and later they can help us. Trusting admits the good in people. African-Americans need to feel solidarity; without trust, there is none.

On this day, I will choose one likely person and begin the long process of forging an alliance based on trust.

March 25

WHITE PEOPLE

If I stepped back and thought about it, I wouldn't be able to do what I do and deal with the type of people I deal with. Because I deal with a lot of white people.

—MAURICE STARR

...And with some success, given Starr's reported net worth in 1991 of $100 million.

When we are clear about our priorities, secure in our identity, and committed to our goals, we can achieve our dreams. Bigotry belongs to others, unless we stew and sputter over it so long that we make it ours, too. We need to find ways to deal with the insensitivity of others so that we can accomplish what we set out to in the short-term without spontaneously combusting years down the line.

Dealing with whites is not the only route to success, but if we take that route, we need to guard against intolerance and insensitivity—theirs *and* ours.

On this day, I will take five minutes to visualize myself calmly negotiating the waters toward accomplishing one of my goals.

March 26

SELF-DETERMINATION

The Negro was invented in America.
                    —JOHN OLIVER KILLENS

Slavery required some creative redefining. Our people were brought here—mothers, fathers, sons and daughters—and were dubbed savages. Savages became slaves and slaves became colored or Negro, no matter the European blood that was now mixed with African and Native American blood in our veins.

Whatever we became, others wrote our definition, or liked to think they did.

Of course, we've always had our own dictionary, which has grown thicker as we have learned about the culture that was stripped from us, and about our efforts in the face of death, fate, and extraordinary oppression. We are defining ourselves as a people and as individuals. Let *us* invent ourselves, know ourselves, and respect ourselves.

On this day, I will take five minutes to be quiet and listen to my inner self, and determine who I am and what I should be.

DIPLOMACY

You worry too much about what goes into your mouth and not enough about what comes out of it.

—LEAH CHASE

Sticks and stones may break bones, but words can cut to the core. Words are more powerful than we realize. Mere words can convince a child that he is worthless and unloved. Mere words can put an unbridgeable distance between spouses. Mere words can stop us in our career paths.

We can probably all recall a time when somebody said something hurtful to us. Long past the apology, if there was one, the words linger on, perhaps still having the power to make us wince. Let's remember that *our* words have the same power.

Let's use our words wisely. They can challenge, but in a positive way. They can praise and encourage and speak with love. Let's use them to build up, rather than destroy.

On this day, I will try to select my words with care, opting for silence rather than abusiveness. And I will remember to affirm my friends and loved ones.

IMPEDIMENTS

*I tell my students there is such a thing as
"writer's block," and they should respect it. It's
blocked because it ought to be blocked, because
you haven't got it right now.*

—TONI MORRISON

Writers or not, there are times when all of us are
"blocked." Our dilemma may be an unsatisfying career or a general feeling of discontent in our daily
lives. We may feel stymied as to what action to take
or what direction to move in. Our indecisiveness may
feel scary or alarming, especially if we are normally
focused and productive people.

The hardest decision may be just to recognize
the block and go with it. We can use it as a time to
weigh our options, determine the possibilities. The
trick is to come out of the block with a renewed sense
of energy and an enthusiastic commitment to taking
our next step.

Our "blocks" are opportunities to grow, to
"write" our futures as we would like them written.
*On this day, I will take five minutes to remember a
time when I felt stuck, and I will visualize coming out
of it and moving on to something better.*

IMAGINATION

*Dream big dreams! Others may deprive you of
your material wealth and cheat you in a
thousand ways, but no man can deprive you of
the control and use of your imagination.*

—JESSE JACKSON

Many of us devalue our imaginations or curb them
because we fear they will tantalize us with impossible
visions. Perhaps our parents or friends made us feel
embarrassed about our "wild imagination." We may
have to learn as adults how to give our imagination
full rein so that we can find those things in life that
will make our time here meaningful and rewarding.

When we combine imagination with determi-
nation and resourcefulness, our dreams become
reality.

*On this day, I will take five minutes to visualize
attaining one of my goals, and I will spend the last
couple of minutes imagining that I exceeded my goals
beyond my wildest imagination.*

March 30

SAVING MONEY

Save money and money will save you.
—JAMAICAN proverb

Everywhere we look, we are admonished to spend, spend, spend!

Living beyond our means can become a very bad habit. It can really demoralize us when it keeps us from taking the steps mature adults ought to be able to manage—finding a secure and pleasant living environment for our children, saving for college and old age, being properly insured.

Let's learn how to handle our money wisely. Even if we can manage to save only a few dollars each week (or month), it's a step in the right direction. Perhaps we can plunge into the task of unloading our debt if we apply our creativity and our energy.

On this day, I will take at least one step to bettering my financial situation. I might take a book on money management out of the library, create a household budget, or look into ways to augment my income.

March 31

WELL-BEING

Hair and teeth—a man got those two things,
he's got it all.

—JAMES BROWN

Just a little levity today!

Throughout this book, we talk of the importance of persevering, of being courageous, of working hard toward all our goals. But we ought not to feel weighted down all the time with the seriousness of our tasks and with our personal struggles. We must occasionally step back to acknowledge how fortunate we are. Even when the hair and teeth are gone—or we can put them on our dresser top at bedtime—we do have so much going for us!

Let's take the opportunity to acknowledge all the good in our lives—the things that make us laugh and make us proud.

At the end of this day, I will remember at least one
good thing that happened to me or consider at least
one thing I have going for me.

PACING

There's no need to hurry, yet no time to lose.
—BESSIE COPAGE

Very often, we're glancing left and right to see how everybody else is doing. When we note that a friend has gotten a job, a promotion, or a pay raise, or is planning to marry or to buy a house, we get antsy. Shouldn't we be farther along?

We have to go at our own pace. What we see happening to others might inspire us to work harder in order to hurry along the prizes and recognition—no harm in that, as long as we don't become frantic or sloppy. There are also times our natural rhythm will tell us to kick back for a while; that can be productive, too.

Let's trust our internal clocks. We all progress at different rates. Comparisons can be demoralizing. There is no "standard time" for human growth and achievement.

On this day, I will do at least one thing that will advance me toward achieving one of my goals.

April 2

BEING BLACK

I've always been proud to be black. But proud and obsessive are different things.

—JACOB LAMAR

Indeed, our pride grows as we learn more about our heritage. Sometimes, we border on becoming obsessed. It's not hard to understand, given how often we're reminded of our "otherness."

Developing a positive image of ourselves has been a necessity. The important thing is not to allow our pride to become a substitute for action.

"I don't need to prove myself; I'm from a great heritage" can be a ruinous attitude if it stops us from functioning. Let's make sure our pride fuels us to make a difference.

On this day, I will take five minutes to look at something speaking to my pride in my heritage—my "X" cap, my family photos, African cloth—and let its lingering mental image inspire me to excellence.

April 3

CREATIVITY

Do a common thing in an uncommon way.
—BOOKER T. WASHINGTON

Creativity is in all of us. People think that if they cannot attack a canvas like Romare Bearden or Jean-Michel Basquiat, if they cannot pen a novel like Alice Walker or Toni Morrison, they are not creative.

Great joy comes from doing things "in an uncommon way." Creativity exercises our minds; it means flouting convention and finding new ways to express ourselves and solve our problems.

We must guard against self-censorship and allow our innate creativity to flourish. Let's dare to put our personal stamp on the things we do and the ways we live.

On this day, I will take two minutes to come up with five new ways to accomplish my goals. The wilder the better; I will just let my inhibitions down.

April 4

CONSIDERATION

*Our society allows people to be absolutely
neurotic and totally out of touch with their
feelings and everyone else's feelings, and yet be
very respectable.*

—NTOZAKE SHANGE

Our professional accomplishments are one thing, but
we often take them to be the *whole* thing, or the only
thing that matters. There is so much more to life.
Let us not focus solely on our careers and acquisi-
tions, but on our achievements as human beings. Let
us look at the way we treat our spouses, our children,
our friends, our community, and ourselves. When we
learn to nourish and nurture and not just consume,
we become more "whole." We acquire *inner* respect-
ability, a goal far worthier than all the window dressing we can manage.

*On this day, I pledge to do something nice for a
colleague or a loved one, or to call or write a "thank
you" letter to someone who has helped me.*

April 5

MIND POWER

It is the mind that makes the body.
—SOJOURNER TRUTH

Life is fraught with challenges; these days life feels more challenging than ever. Stress can cripple us, wreaking havoc with our ability to meet the challenges daily life throws our way.

Many of us claim we'd like to lose a few pounds or tone up our bodies, get fit and become more energetic. But how many of us realize that it's our mind—not our genes, our sweet tooth, our life-style, or Mom's cooking—that ultimately inspires or sabotages us.

When we are mentally strong and committed, we can do anything. So how do we "bulk up" our minds? As with a muscle: by constant flexing with positive thoughts. Professional athletes can attest to the necessity of psychological stamina. Get the mind in shape and the body will follow.

On this day, I will take five minutes to relax and visualize myself accomplishing one of my goals.

April 6

STRUGGLE

You cannot fight by being on the outside
complaining and whining. You have to get on
the inside to be able to assess their strengths
and weaknesses and then move in.

—SHIRLEY CHISHOLM

Outward appearances are often deceiving. We might look at a company, for example, and view it as a supremely productive monolith. When we step inside and become part of the organization, however, we might be amazed to note its chaos.

We must strive to get inside the door more often—in government, in business, in all sorts of endeavors and organizations—in order to advance. We might learn that it's often more a person's will than her ability that enables her to succeed.

On this day, I will take five minutes to reflect on an
obstacle I might encounter in accomplishing my goal.
Then I will come up with at least one way around or
through that obstacle.

LOVE

I have cared for more than six hundred addicted babies since we opened the center. . . . They love you to tell them how great they are, how good they are. Somehow, even at a young age, they understand that.

—CLARA "MOTHER" HALE

Positive reinforcement is something we all need. Children develop their sense of self-worth at an early age, so it is vital to let them know how much we treasure them. We can praise their crayoned scribbles, listen and respond to their attempts at expressing themselves, respect their feelings, and encourage their interests. We can be ready with a hug and kiss.

Even in adulthood, we need to feel appreciated and loved, but sometimes we withhold our approval of others because we are jealous of them or insecure. We say we don't want to give someone a "big head." But in an indifferent, sometimes hostile, world, who couldn't use more support?

On this day, I will make a special point of complimenting and affirming African-Americans, young and old.

April 8

BUILDING

Our children may learn about heroes of the past. Our task is to make ourselves architects of the future.

—JOMO KENYATTA

It is not enough to point to the heroes of our struggle and simply expect our children to absorb and mimic their exemplary qualities. We have an obligation to see to it that the future holds promise and opportunities.

As architects of the future of African-Americans, we must accept the burden of fighting the fights that need to be fought now, of making inroads where we can, so that our children have a better place from which to start.

On this day, I will do at least one thing that advances me toward one of my goals.

April 9

FAILURE

*I don't believe in failure. It is not failure if
you enjoyed the process.*

—OPRAH WINFREY

In a lifetime of striving to fulfill ourselves, our efforts
do not always meet with resounding success. But
what appears to the world as failure does not have to
be that for us. If we start up a shoe store and soon
close it and go bankrupt, have we failed? To others
it might seem so, but that is a simplistic reading of
the situation. We have probably learned a whole lot
about setting up shop, and so our efforts contribute
to our growth. If we have learned, we have not failed.
Enjoying the process ensures that no matter the outcome, we'll not be deterred in future efforts.

*On this day, I will take five minutes to remember
that all my past endeavors—even if I have committed
mistakes while implementing them—have been
successes; they have given me valuable experience for
myself and experience that I can pass on to other
African-Americans.*

April 10

READING

It often requires more courage to read some books than it does to fight a battle.

—SUTTON E. GRIGGS

How many of us would say we make adequate time for reading in our lives? Reading can help us clarify our confusion and enhance our perspective. Books and newspapers show us other worlds, other experiences, and unlike television, allow us the time and the silence to absorb and to question. We may not agree with what a writer is saying, but even then we've learned something about ourselves or discovered how to articulate our own thoughts.

On this day, I will make time to read a chapter of a fiction or nonfiction book, or a selection of poetry.

April 11

COMMUNICATION

We're living in an age when people need to talk. They don't communicate.

—QUEEN LATIFAH

We sometimes refuse to talk because we think that nobody will listen. Other times we utter commands or accusations, but we're not in the mood for discussion; we've already made up our minds and we won't be challenged. We may consciously or unconsciously hope to intimidate, so we bark or bleat or curse or rant—anything but really talk.

Telling someone to "shut up" or shouting an insult does nothing but wound and provoke resentment. Not to imply we shouldn't get angry, but if we never articulate our desires, frustrations, resentment, or hurts, how can we hope to resolve matters? When we take the time to explain ourselves, to our families or to people of different backgrounds, we can open up a dialogue that results in positive change.

On this day, I will visualize myself communicating effectively at work or at home rather than being silent or simply venting hostility.

PRIVATE TIME

*We shouldn't depend on the outside world for
our happiness; we should have our private world
where we go for some peace. So we must be
careful about how we build our private worlds.*

— J. CALIFORNIA COOPER

Let's take one minute to examine our private worlds.
What do we find there that nurtures us, that gives
us pleasure or satisfaction? Have we even allowed
ourselves a private world, or are we totally dependent
on other people to give our lives meaning?

Sometimes it appears we are quick to fill up
our alone time with people and noise and commo-
tion—anything to avoid those moments alone. But
it's through the private times we have with ourselves
that we can learn to enjoy our own company. Maybe
it's the way our hands work when we tinker with our
car, put up a batch of preserves, knit a sweater, or
tend to our herb garden that gives us pleasure. We
are all many-faceted people, but we may never get to
know ourselves fully if we don't focus some time and
energy on ourselves.

*On this day, I will give myself the time to do
something that is meaningful and pleasurable to me.*

April 13

TIMING

The best time to do a thing is when it can be done.
—WILLIAM PICKENS

Many of us procrastinate, putting off a task until we wince when we're reminded of it. Others do the opposite, rushing into things without proper preparation. Both approaches usually meet with failure.

We must find the right time to act. It may be frustrating to wait; we may fear that we'll lose our edge. Sometimes it's the smartest thing. The executive we're approaching with a proposal may be more kindly disposed to us after he's had a chance to settle in after his two-week vacation.

Very often we have a number of things demanding action. We have to determine our priorities and start at the top of the list. Cleaning our closets can wait till our work or school assignment is completed.

On this day, I will take five minutes to organize my priorities, determining what can wait and what needs to be done immediately.

April 14

LOVE

*I've heard some of the young people laugh
about slave love, but they should envy the love
which kept mother and father so close together
in life, and even held them in death.*

*—ALONZO HAYWOOD,
former enslaved African-American*

◼||||◼||||◼

Romantic love is one of life's precious bouquets to
us. It has the power to endure all sorts of hardships
and disappointments that come our way. But for love
to last, we must nurture it. That can be difficult
when we are besieged by the demands of work and
children. A strong commitment may endure brief
stretches of inattention, but eventually requires our
notice. We need to be creative in finding ways to
focus on one another. Small gestures say "I love
you".—a back rub, a museum postcard with a warm
message tucked inside a briefcase, or a surprise weekend breakfast in bed.

*On this day, I will make some small gesture of
affection to a special person in my life.*

April 15

PURPOSE

Little by little the bird makes it nest.
—HAITIAN *proverb*

How many of us would describe ourselves as patient? Usually we're the first to admit that we are impatient for success, for advancement in our careers, or for finding lasting love. If patience *is* in short supply, how do we hang in there to reach our goals?

A sense of purpose helps. At Kwanzaa, we celebrate Nia, or purpose, with which we focus on our goals. While the steps we take may seem small and insignificant, we need to keep in mind the larger picture that will inspire us to keep moving forward. There is a story of two stonemasons. When asked what he was doing, the first replied, "Making a brick." When the second was asked, he answered, "Building a cathedral."

On this day, I will make at least one concrete gesture toward accomplishing one of my goals.

April 16

SELF-RESPECT

If you respect yourself, it's easier to respect other people.

—JOHN SINGLETON

When we start disliking ourselves for our weaknesses and shortcomings, we can't resist putting down everybody else, particularly those who threaten us.

We've got to learn to like and respect ourselves, regardless of our faults. This may require rejecting destructive criticisms our parents gave us as children and breaking the habit of knocking ourselves. Our efforts and our dreams can help restore our flagging self-respect, and then we'll be able to approach others without the need to belittle them.

On this day, I will take five minutes to note and appreciate the good things about myself.

COMPULSIVENESS

When do any of us ever do enough?
—BARBARA JORDAN

The fact is, compulsiveness is seldom rewarded because it can never be sated. The person who thinks that there is always more to do, that there can never be *enough*, is bound to be frustrated.

There are times when, simply, enough is enough. When we have worked hard enough, waited long enough, loved enough. Perhaps we are involved in a difficult relationship and we have done everything we can think of to make it work. We can cheat ourselves if we hold on to something that reason tells us is unworkable. In a job where we have given our all and yet had our efforts unrecognized, we can say, "Time to move on."

We must know that in certain instances, we *have* done enough. Now, if you want to talk about African-Americans doing more to help ourselves—yes, this is one area where we can never do enough!

On this day, I pledge to give all I can to a given task in the time allotted, and when it is finished, I will move on to the next project.

April 18

SELF-DETERMINATION

Acceptance of prevailing standards often means
we have no standards of our own.

—JEAN TOOMER

When we allow others to think for us, we surrender
a piece of ourselves. Doing what is "cool" can be
dangerous. We *must* think for ourselves.

By being true to ourselves—our conscience
and emotions—we avoid having to change ourselves
whenever the people around us change. That may
entail taking a moral stance that is unpopular and
consequently it demands inner strength and
resolution.

We must first learn to think—to sort things
through, question, analyze, decide our values and
opinions. When we can articulate them, if only to
ourselves, we can know ourselves and be true to
ourselves.

On this day, I will take five minutes and remember a
time when I had the courage of my convictions and
did not go with the crowd.

April 19

AMBITION

*I stood up in front of a speech class and said,
"I plan to make my living with my oratory
skills, and I'd like to be a talk show host."
There was a pause, then the most incredible
laughter you've ever heard in your life.*

—ARSENIO HALL

When we desire a grand achievement, we have to be
prepared to face ridicule. We need to have the guts
to stand up to that.

Perhaps we cope by keeping our real dreams
close to our vest. Others of us might enjoy the challenge of stating our goals publicly so that we are
driven to prove our seriousness.

Let's allow ourselves to dream as big, as mon-
umental, as we want. Let no one else cut our dreams
down to size.

*On this day, I will take five minutes and visualize
that I have accomplished one of my goals. I will feel,
see, and hear in detail how my life will change once I
have accomplished it.*

April 20

MORTALITY

I never thought I would live to be forty....
I am stronger for confronting the hard
issue of breast cancer, of mortality, dying.
—AUDRE LORDE

Most of us do not relish contemplating our mortality. Few of us would say that we've accomplished what we hoped to in our lives, and while we may be proud of our efforts thus far—as a parent or a child, a friend or a spouse, a teacher or a social worker—we have a lot more to do!

Let's treasure each moment that we have, because tomorrow is not guaranteed. Let's not waste our lives in fear or anger or pain, but break free of all constrictions to live in a way that fulfills us. Let's express what we feel we need to, and do the things that reward us. Life is too short to waste, and time can never be recaptured.

On this day, I will take five minutes to think about what I need to do to make my life satisfying, and I will then pledge to do what it takes.

April 21

FULFILLMENT

*A few years ago, I just thought about winning.
When I won, I was happy and when I lost, I
was unhappy. Now I am happy in my
circumstances, even when I lose. That's my
decision, not an excuse, because I like how I
am and what I'm doing.*

—YANNICK NOAH

When we derive pleasure from our daily lives, are
stimulated or challenged by our work, enriched by
the new things we learn and by our contact with others, our lives are successful regardless of the specific
setbacks of a particular day. Instead of cataloguing
disappointments, let's make a mental computation
of all the things that make us happy and proud and
that gratify us. When we like who we are and what
we're doing, we are winners at the biggest game—
life!

*At the end of this day, I will remember at least one
good thing that happened to me, or something I did
that gave me pleasure or satisfaction.*

April 22

CONTRIBUTING

*I believe in helping people the best way you
can; my way is through my art. But sometimes
you need a splash of cold water in your face to
make you see the right way to do it.*

—ARTHUR MITCHELL

We don't all need to be civil-rights leaders or lawyers
to help. That splash of cold water can awaken us to
the best way we can put our own natural talents and
ambitions to use. There are some who teach, some
who blaze trails, some who acquire power that will be
wielded on our behalf. Let us refrain from blasting
those who are contributing in subtler ways; we may
have assumed self-centeredness where there is so
much more.

What is so valuable—and we often downplay
or ignore this—is to give our children confidence,
enthusiasm, and the ability to dream. And if we
never become parents ourselves, we still have an obligation to "our children," to the future of African-
American people.

*On this day, I will do at least one thing that will help
me advance toward one of my goals.*

BALANCE

I try to balance my life. When I'm home, I give quality time.... I'm happy I've achieved what I have without losing my head.

—PATTI LABELLE

Managing our lives can be tricky. We may not have the neatly ordered life-style that makes for simple scheduling. At any point in our life, health, child-rearing, or career may require our overwhelming attention, causing other areas to dangle for a while, neglected. Some of us are "too busy" to make time for friends, get necessary medical checkups and examinations (like mammograms), evaluate our children's schoolwork, or address our decreasing fitness. We end up trusting that, for a while, things will "hold," that nothing will go wildly askew.

Maintaining our physical, spiritual, and mental health requires some juggling; there may be no "perfect" balance so we need to be reasonable and forgiving.

On this day, I will take five minutes to think about the balance of activities, things, and people in my life.

April 24

ALIENATION

Half the time I feel like I'm on the outside of the world peeping in through a knot-hole in the fence.

—RICHARD WRIGHT, from Native Son

Feelings of alienation can visit us all, and they sometimes move in for an extended stay. It may seem at times that all the action is "out there" somewhere, and that we're no more than observers. Perhaps we feel incapable of plunging in, competing, fighting, making our mark on the world.

What choice do we really have? If we withdraw, we lose out on chances to give ourselves the rewards and satisfactions that are possible.

Our interaction with others can make a positive impact. Let's understand that who we are is what we've decided we'll be. Let's recognize our personal power. We have more control than we may think.

On this day, I will do something to involve myself— at work, in the PTA, or with my family. I will make my voice heard.

April 25

MULTIFACETEDNESS

*I knew that if a music career wasn't going
to happen, I could do other things to make my
contribution—medicine was one, and I was also
interested in law.*

—BARBARA HENDRICKS

Obviously, we want to focus our energy in one direction at a time or else we dilute our abilities by
scattering our efforts. Barbara Hendricks did concentrate on singing opera. Still, it's beneficial to
know that there are many fields in which we are capable and in which we can succeed.

*On this day, no matter how happy I may be, I will
take five minutes to remember that I have many
options. I am not bound to one course alone and can
change direction if I so desire.*

April 26

PREJUDICE

*I believe in recognizing every human being
as a human being—neither white, black, brown,
or red.*

—MALCOLM X

To most of us, what Malcolm X referred to in his
autobiography could take place only in an ideal
world. And certainly American society is still a long
way from joining hands and singing "Kumbaya" together. Nevertheless, we of African descent must remember that being proud of our African heritage
means at least *trying* to live up to the highest ideals
of our traditions. That means supplanting falsehood
with truth, not other falsehoods; it means supplanting intolerance with tolerance, not further intolerance. It means that we try our best, using the
guideposts of our great heritage, to make a better
world.

*On this day, I will take five minutes to think about
negative stereotypes or antagonisms I may hold about
other ethnic groups. I will reflect upon whether these
feelings are helping me accomplish my own goals or
are contributing to my overall happiness.*

April 27

POTENTIAL

A mind is a terrible thing to waste.
—THE UNITED NEGRO COLLEGE FUND

Isn't that the truth. And it can be depressing seeing some of our finest youngsters not living up to their potential. But we need not feel powerless. We must try to be a living example ourselves. We must encourage all African-American children, whether or not we are related to them, to follow their dreams. And, if we can, we should give generously of our time and money to provide scholarships to help make their dreams become reality.

On this day I will do my best to affirm the ambitions and dreams of my fellow African-Americans, especially children.

April 28

STRUGGLE

If murderers come to kill you, you do not say,
"I cannot oppose the next stab wound because
my life is already forfeit." No—you fight for
your life!

—HERMON GEORGE, JR.

No matter how much we may have been wounded—
by the blows dealt us through our educational or political systems—we cannot give up. As soon as we
surrender, the forces of oppression win. More to the
point, we lose.

Certainly there may be times when we just
don't want to fight anymore. Prejudice's army is
large and seems to be constantly replenished, generation after generation. How can we sustain our
energy?

It helps to know that our people are there on
the front lines with us. When we are wounded, we
must yell out for help. And when we hear the cry of
others in despair, we must rush to their aid.

On this day, I will turn my attention to a friend, a
relative, or a stranger who is struggling and see what
I can do to help.

April 29

SUCCESS

I used to want the words "She tried" on my tombstone. Now I want "She did it."

—KATHERINE DUNHAM

How glorious an inscription—She did it! Some of us may have to content ourselves with "She tried," but who really wants the words "She gave up" to mark her departure?

Most of us get to spend a decent number of years on this planet, which means we really ought to figure out what's important to us. If we find the things we love to do, our years will be rewarding and, when we exit, we'll do so with a sense of fulfillment, of good memories and time well spent.

When we apply ourselves to the ideas and values we hold important, we are already living "successfully." If we've held to our commitments to the best of our ability, we can congratulate ourselves at the end of every day with "I did it!"

On this day, I will do at least one concrete thing that advances me toward one of my goals.

April 30

RELATIONSHIPS

I know now that no other woman can take the place of a man's mother, and that no man can take the place of a woman's father.

—QUINCY JONES

Some of us are guilty of expecting our mates to live up to the inspiring example of our mother or father. When our partner fails to do so, we feel let down.

A few of these relationships may work, but we are forced to acknowledge that no one can fill the shoes of another. It's unfair to expect a romantic partner to assume a parental role or compete with our idealized image of Mom or Dad.

The needy child may linger in us, but we need to find other ways to assuage our pain.

On this day, I will take five minutes to think about my spouse or significant other; I will note what there is about him or her that is unique, and I will appreciate those qualities.

QUESTIONING

*All over the world, nobody has a God who
doesn't resemble them. Except black Americans.
They can't even see they're worshipping
someone else's God, because they want so badly
to assimilate.*

—AUGUST WILSON

It is no easy matter to challenge the concepts and
messages that have been ingrained in us. Perhaps we
are uneasy about challenging authority, whether of
our church or of our parents. Perhaps we have no
better wisdom to supplant what we suspect is invalid
or inappropriate for us.

We need to accept that periods of instability
and confusion come with growth. We should also
know that change just for the sake of change can
ultimately backfire on us as easily as benefit us. Let's
accept the risks of questioning, because the risks of
blind acceptance are even greater.

*On this day, I will choose one thing or idea I take for
granted. Then I will take five minutes to imagine the
possibilities if that given didn't exist or were the exact
opposite of what it seems today.*

May 2

SELF-CONFIDENCE

If you have no confidence in self, you are twice defeated in the race of life. With confidence, you have won even before you have started.

—MARCUS GARVEY

We hear about self-confidence all our lives. We may wonder, "Do I have it? Can I get some?"

Self-confidence, contrary to rumor, is not a thing that either you're born with or you're out of luck. It can and should be developed. Self-confidence does not necessarily spread to all facets of a person, either. A supremely self-confident businessman may crumble when faced with the prospect of losing twenty pounds. A top-notch lawyer may get the shakes trying to make heads or tails out of her tax forms.

We all have our unique talents and virtues. Taking stock of them is vital so that we can reinforce our sense of self-worth and carry it over into other, less-sure areas of our lives.

On this day, I will remember a time when someone told me I couldn't accomplish something—and I proved him wrong.

NETWORKING

A single bracelet does not jingle.

—CONGO *proverb*

Some of us, especially when we are young, are under the mistaken impression that whatever our endeavor, we've got to go it alone. We make it a point of honor not to ask for help. But it is seldom that *anyone* does *anything* alone. This especially holds for those who seem most favored; Ivy League alums have no compunction about making a few phone calls to secure Junior an interview with the company president.

There are African-Americans who have achieved success and are approachable and willing to help; we must make an effort to search them out. And we need not shy away from soliciting guidance from and making alliances with persons of any ethnicity. Contacts count, and we quickly learn that we can make a bit more noise with a few more business cards.

On this day, I will choose one likely person, and begin the long process of forging an alliance based on trust with him or her. Or I will suggest to someone I am beginning to trust that we get together over coffee.

May 4

OBSTACLES

*We must use time creatively . . . and forever
realize that the time is always ripe to do right.*
—MARTIN LUTHER KING, JR.

▰▰▰▰▰▰

Once in a while we like to convince ourselves that
we've missed the boat. It's just too late to do anything about it, we say. Maybe it's too late to patch
up an ailing relationship; too late to forge a closer
bond with our child; too late to go back to school;
too late to make a career change. When we tell ourselves this, we take the easy way out, because to act
requires energy and effort. To act also poses a risk
of failure.

Why not assume success instead of failure and
let that inspire us to work toward our goal. "How
can I do this?" are magic words when issued in a
positive frame of mind.

*On this day, I will take five minutes to reflect on an
obstacle I might encounter in accomplishing my goal.
Then I will come up with at least one way around or
through that obstacle.*

ENVY

*Do not despise or hate your neighbor because he
has been a success; take care of your own case.*
— WILLIAM T. VERNON

What more useless emotion is there than envy? It is
an interesting fact that we often don't even recognize
that we have fallen victim to that green-eyed
monster.

Example: A friend lands a prestigious new job,
earning what must be a handsome wage. What do we
do? Give her a pat on the back, then turn around
and think smugly, "That company stinks; she'll
never go higher than where she is now." We diminish
her accomplishment, write it off to luck, or belittle
her in other respects—her looks or her love life.

Maybe it makes us feel better—temporarily.
Days later we're still bemoaning our awful luck. All
this time spent unproductively. How much more affirming to let our friend's success inspire us to
achieve our own. Envy divides us, and our people can
ill afford to be divided.

*On this day, I pledge to learn by others' successes
and commit my own successes to help others.*

May 6

PREPARATION

You cannot shave a man's head in his absence.
—*YORUBA proverb*

If there's something we want to do, we need to have all the elements present. In this case—the man with hair on his head, the razor, water, the shaving lather.

Whatever we attempt in life, there is work entailed in gathering together all the elements necessary for our success. If we want to get in better health, we must first have a mental commitment to our goal. We're also going to require some nutrition information, some exercise guidance, perhaps a doctor's checkup. It requires some planning. Ambition alone is not enough.

As much as possible, we must *learn* what we'll need to do so we can increase our chances of success. Let's not overlook the importance of planning.

On this day, I will make a list of the things I need to know and do to accomplish one of my goals.

SLOGANEERING

*I'd rather see a cat with a processed head
and a natural mind than a natural head and a
processed mind.*

—H. RAP BROWN

We cried out against taking the processed package of
history and culture we learned at school and accepting it as the total package. Still, we are not always
successful at recognizing the processed thought that
often has been amusingly or provokingly sloganized.
We make song lyrics or movie dialogue or political
sound bites into neat emblems that we wear on our
sleeve until a new one comes along to tickle us or
make us feel righteous. If anger is the faddish sentiment, we're angry.

Let's determine our own thoughts, to make
sure that what comes out is genuine.

*On this day, I will take five minutes to look at
something speaking to my pride in my heritage—my
"X" cap, African cloth—and let its lingering inner
meaning, rather than its fashionable visual or verbal
slogan, inspire me to excellence.*

May 8

ANGER

*Anger is an emotion that if you carry around
over a long period of time, it doesn't allow you
to live.*

—JOHN SINGLETON

African-Americans know about anger because we
know about injustice and inhumanity. When we
cling to our anger, however, it can prevent us from
experiencing our lives with the greatest possible joy
and contentment. Anger squelches happiness; it
feeds upon itself to the point where it distorts our
vision of life.

Okay, we may *feel* angry, but let's not condition ourselves always to *respond* with anger. Anger
can be lethal, because it can kill a vital part of ourselves and cheat us of life's very real and rewarding
possibilities.

*On this day, if I get angry with something or
someone, I will acknowledge that anger, but then I
will let it dissipate and get on with what I am trying
to accomplish.*

May 9

INDEPENDENCE

*We had a strong relationship based on mutual respect and love. I had to go through a difficult struggle, searching for someone to replace her, someone who could say, "Never mind, this is what's important." I finally found that **person** in myself.*

—BARBARA HENDRICKS

There may come a time in our lives where we find ourselves very attached to a mentor. Singer Barbara Hendricks found that guidance and devotion in her vocal coach, mezzo-soprano Jennie Tourel. It can be frightening, then, when we suddenly find ourselves alone—as Hendricks did after Tourel's death—with no sounding board to help us make our choices or reinforce our egos.

We can gratefully accept guidance, but let's always keep our hands on the rudder so that if conditions change we are still able to navigate on our own.

On this day, I will remember that I can take advice and guidance from others, but that the ultimate decision will be mine.

May 10

PROBLEMS

When it rains, the roof always drips the same way.
—JABO proverb

In human behavior, patterns exist. If we are observant, we can spot them.

Example 1: Our last three relationships never got further than the first date and we're baffled. Perhaps, if we looked closely, we might see that we came on way too strong and scared our potential suitors away. We'll slow down in the future.

Example 2: This is the second job we've had and hated. Let's first find out why. Is it a particular task or set of tasks common to both that we dislike?

After determining the cause of the trouble, let's then be ready to pull out the tools we need and get to work.

On this day, I will spend five minutes and target one thing that is preventing me from accomplishing one of my goals. Then I will visualize myself overcoming that problem.

PLEASURE

While I can't say there was a particular moment when I attended a concert, heard a piece and was overwhelmed, music was always around, and I just sang for the pleasure of it.
— BARBARA HENDRICKS

How much do we do for the pure pleasure of it? We exercise with a goal in mind of losing weight or toning up. We cook to give the kids their nutrition. We work for a paycheck. We bathe to get clean.

In all our running around and striving to secure a certain kind of life for ourselves and our families, we often neglect our need for pleasure. Sure, pursuit of pleasure should not interfere with our ability to pay the tuition, the rent, or the orthodontist. But without some pleasure in our lives, we are soon overwhelmed by the drudgery.

On this day, I will take five minutes to consider what I can do to add more pleasure to my life.

May 12

SELF-DETERMINATION

I'd continue to teach my children what I had been taught: that they needn't see a black become president or win the Indy 500 on television before they could do it in real life.

—ERIC V. COPAGE

It's good to have role models. We ought to be able to look at television and see ourselves, to have our presence acknowledged and our abilities noted. Role models can help our children see that any dream is possible.

But to put our dreams at the mercy of a few television programmers is a mistake. Had earlier generations of our people done so, we would have been doomed; there would not be any African-American doctors, lawyers, teachers, entrepreneurs, and scholars. We must be the ones to program our present and our future, because how we see ourselves is infinitely more important than how others see us or depict us.

On this day, I will strive to do my job, no matter what it is, as best I can. And I pledge today to encourage and support friends and other African-Americans in their endeavors.

May 13

AMBITION

The ladder of success is never crowded at the top.
—FLORENCE GRIFFITH JOYNER

There are times when we look up and cannot even begin to make out the top of the ladder of success; perhaps that is the time to look down and see how far we've already come, or, instead, to look only as far as the next rung.

When we acknowledge that no one's energy and effort is required but ours, we can climb as long as it takes to claim our spot at the top of the ladder—but let's remember to reach down to help others on the way up.

On this day, I will do at least one thing that advances me toward the attainment of one of my goals.

May 14

SELF-WORTH

*A man's vocation is no measure for his inner
feelings nor a guarantee of his earnest desire to
live right and attain the highest standards.*
—JACK JOHNSON

Do we want to live well? Of course we do. But what
does that mean to us? Financial success is one goal,
but sometimes it supersedes all other ambitions.
When we swallow the standards of our generation,
we lose track of what it takes to make our own life
meaningful.

Let's proceed carefully when we attempt to as-
cribe value to our choices, and to others' choices as
well. Buying into the going "ideal" might mean
we've sold our standards.

Our checkbook balance indicates we are clever
at making money; it doesn't bestow moral dignity or
esteem. For that, we take a reading of the heart,
mind, and soul of a person—things not so obviously
discernible.

*On this day, I will take five minutes to be quiet,
listen to my inner self, and determine who I am and
who I want to be.*

STRESS

Excessive or prolonged stress, particularly in the form of frustration, fear or anxiety, is distress, and it leads to disease.

—GAIL C. CHRISTOPHER

Life is not simple. We find ourselves saddled with all kinds of worries, too numerous to mention, which affect all areas of our lives, from our personal safety, to our job and financial worries, to our romantic and family relationships. Each worry, whether acknowledged or buried, exacts its share of damage upon our system. When we do nothing to fortify our bodies to live and deal with stress, our bodies and minds pay the price.

On this day, I will take the time to find some way to relax, whether it be taking a bath, meditating, or exercising.

May 16

LOSING

Losses always attend moving.
—CHARLES V. ROMAN

We go through life trying valiantly to think of ourselves as winners. Perhaps that's why the disappointment is so great when we lose. What do we do to remind ourselves that we're still winners, especially when the evidence of our recent failure begins to cast doubts?

Even winning teams have losses, we must remember. It's what we *do* with our losses that counts. Interviewed after the game, the players on the losing team seem to know what went wrong; they rattle off their weaknesses and make note of the other team's strengths.

As long as we're living and striving to reach our goals, we'll know loss, failure, setbacks. It's only when we stop trying that we defeat ourselves.

On this day, I will take five minutes to remember a time when I failed. Then I will reflect on why I failed. Then I will visualize attempting the same goal, making adjustments, and succeeding this time.

May 17

LOVE

To love is to make of one's heart a swinging door.
—HOWARD THURMAN

Loving well requires our being able to accept love as well as give it. It's easy to see that we cannot just be "takers," but some of us may have problems with the opposite, having learned that "it is better to give than to receive."

Yet too much love that is too furiously focused can smother the object of our affections. We deny our beloved the pleasure and fulfillment of loving and nurturing us. Our lovers want to feel that we need them, too.

Let us be aware of the difference between love and obsession. Obsession is not real love, but closer to addiction. Love that is as happily received as it is given will be stronger and more durable.

On this day, I will take five minutes to imagine or remember a time when someone did something considerate or affectionate toward me. I will imagine receiving that affection with open arms and grace.

May 18

DECISIONS

I taped the application and ironed it.
—DEBI THOMAS

In 1986 champion figure skater Debi Thomas was stretched thin between her college studies and her training. After receiving a C on a chemistry final, feeling exhausted and frustrated, she tore up her application for the United States Figure Skating Championship. As her quote reveals, Debi Thomas changed her mind. She went on to take the women's title.

There are no "decision police" out there to arrest us when we change our minds. No one says we can't retract a statement, reverse a policy, or make a total about-face. We sometimes say and do things out of emotion which, on second thought, we regret. If we can't live with our decisions, let's decide again.

On this day, I will take five minutes to review my life to see what, if any, changes I should make.

May 19

OPENNESS

*To be a great musician, you've got to be open
to what's new, what's happening at the
moment. You have to be able to absorb it if
you're going to continue to grow and
communicate.*

—MILES DAVIS

Life, in all its aspects, is constantly changing, and
we must do our best to stay aware of what's going
on in the world—from politics to popular culture,
from sociology to science and medicine.

When we absorb and talk about what's going
on around us, we are truly alive.

*On this day, I will make an effort to learn something
new, by either reading the newspaper, listening to the
radio, or talking with a friend or co-worker.*

May 20

PERFECTION

No one is perfect in this imperfect world.
— PATRICE LUMUMBA

How often we may have longed for the perfect parents, the perfect mate, the perfect children, or the perfect boss or teacher! What we look for in these perfect people is the ability to be fair and generous with us, to recognize how special we are and help us realize aspects of ourselves we may have trouble seeing.

We are misguided when we pine for perfection. A "perfect opportunity" is such because we apply ourselves to plumb the good we have located, not because of anything inherent in the situation itself. There is always effort involved. We may be guided or inspired by others, but no one person or thing can magically bestow a gift-wrapped package of blessings to still the yearnings of our souls.

On this day, I will look for, or look to create, opportunities that will help me advance toward one of my goals.

May 21

ACCOMMODATION

Living together is an art.
—WILLIAM PICKENS

It's vital that we give some thought to our living arrangements, and vow to practice the arts of compromise and mutual respect. We must show the same common courtesy to those who share our roof that we accord to others. We need to reach agreements on the division of space and labor; imbalances make for eventual problems. We must show respect not only for personal space—and this goes for our children's space, too—but for the overall atmosphere of the home. In our house, tantrums and general grumpiness go into the bedroom until a more serene outlook can emerge.

Living harmoniously in our home enables us to approach the world outside with composure.

On this day, I will take five minutes to meditate on my living situation: Does everyone have enough space and privacy, and if not, what might I do to improve the situation? If I currently live alone, I will think about my living space—is it conducive to what I want to do with my life?

May 22

CHANGE

To change is to be vulnerable.
And to be vulnerable is to be alive.

—ALEXIS DE VEAUX

At the precise moment of change, we might be at once frightened and exhilarated. A new job or career switch will challenge our abilities. A commitment to a relationship will require that we take on certain obligations to our partner. With any change we undertake, we put ourselves in a vulnerable position. We might fail.

We must summon up our courage. When we allow ourselves to change, we become pioneers and explorers. We push our limits, expand our boundaries, take control.

On this day, I will remember a time of transition—a new job, graduation, marriage, my first child—and reexperience the excitement and emotions I had during that event.

May 23

REJECTION

I have learned to take "no" as a vitamin.
—SUZANNE DE PASSE

><><><><

What an irresistible quote, and an encouraging thought. Just as the vitamins we take strengthen us, so can the no's we hear throughout our lives. But notice that even the successful television producer Suzanne de Passe had to *learn* this trick.

How do *we* react when someone tells us no? Do we grudgingly acquiesce or do we look at it as a challenge?

On this day, I will take five minutes to remember a time when somebody told me "No!" and I will visualize my going ahead anyway and succeeding at my goal.

May 24

FLEXIBILITY/DETERMINATION

You can map out a fight plan or a life plan, but when the action starts, it may not go the way you planned, and you're down to your reflexes— which means your training.

—JOE FRAZIER

Let's face it. Things seldom go the way we plan. We have setbacks and stalls. Not everything is within our control. The person who was going to hire/promote us gets canned. Now where are we?

Like a boxer in the ring, we assess the situation and figure out what changes in strategy we need to make in order to win. It is crucial that we not allow ourselves to become demoralized. Read about millionaires: Many of them have had several business failures before their success.

We need to be flexible as well as determined. Let's figure out our plans B and C in case Plan A doesn't work.

On this day, I will take five minutes to think of at least one alternative way to accomplish my goal.

May 25

EFFICIENCY

*If initiative is the ability to do the right thing,
then efficiency is the ability to do the thing
right.*

—KELLY MILLER

Initiative may drive us, but efficiency keeps our
hands on the wheel and our foot appropriately ac-
celerating, slowing, or ready to brake. Without efficiency, we go off the road.

When we are driven, we often focus so much
on achieving our goals that we become reckless.
There are times to go full speed, but also times to
slow down a bit, turn off in a new direction, or pull
over to look at the map and figure out where we are.

*On this day, I will take five minutes to determine
whether I am going about pursuing my goals in the
most efficient manner. And I will pledge to make
changes if necessary.*

PLAY

*It is an emergency for me to learn how to play.
It is something I don't know how to do. I've
never just taken time off and played.*

—BERNICE JOHNSON REAGON

Generally, African-Americans have a healthy attitude about play. We know the restorative qualities it
has; we intuit that it is not only our work that defines us. We can play for the sheer pleasure of it.
Maybe our history here has taught us the importance
of joy in our lives.

Right now, many of us are so busy that we
don't give enough time to play. Nevertheless, playing
is a must for both our mental and physical health.
So let's make time for it, remembering that our individual natures will point us to the tennis court or
the dance floor, to the campground or the bike trail,
to wrestling with our children or with our mates!

*On this day, I will take time to either do something I
enjoy or plan for a future fun excursion, such as
riding a bike trail or going camping.*

May 27

AGGRESSIVENESS

*I had to make my own opportunity. . . . Don't
sit down and wait for the opportunities to come;
you have to get up and make them.*

—MADAME C. J. WALKER

Wouldn't it be great if we could be "discovered"? If
some powerful person could see through to the greatness and specialness inside us and recognize that we
are worthy of fame, fortune, and fulfillment. But
would we really appreciate it as much as we do when
all these follow hard work?

Anyone with a dream or a vision has the responsibility to him- or herself to make that vision
real. Initiative gets us going. Resourcefulness, creativity, and perseverance *keep* us going. When we wait
to be "tapped," we put our achievement in someone
else's hands. We can shape our destiny or let others
find a use for us as they see fit. With the latter
course, we may be lucky. We may not. The choice
should be ours.

*On this day, I will do at least one concrete thing to
advance me toward one of my goals.*

May 28

CREATIVITY

There is a use for almost everything.
—GEORGE WASHINGTON CARVER

. . . Yes, even the lowly little peanut, which had been rather overlooked until Carver got to it.

Our history in this country required us to be ingenious. Today we must use our ingenuity more than ever—in acquiring jobs, making professional advances, and improving our living conditions.

There is not one of us who does not have strengths, talents, and unique abilities. We must nurture them in ourselves and in our children. If we don't, we are wasting the best parts of ourselves.

There is no such thing as an unskilled laborer. Let us determine our skills. The benefits are ours.

On this day, I will take five minutes to focus on my skills. I pledge to develop those skills and to put them to good use.

May 29

SEX

Blacks comprise 14% of New York State's population, but in 1991 comprised 40% of the state's AIDS cases. "AIDS in future generations may be primarily a disease of black people," said Lorna McBarnette, executive deputy commissioner, New York State health department.

—THE NEW YORK TIMES

Scary. But we don't need to accept this as our fate, as McBarnette points out in the article. Acting responsibly is the only answer. Abstinence is obviously the safest way to go, but many of us will find it difficult to commit to that.

Condoms are the next best thing. We cannot let embarrassment keep us from doing what is necessary to decrease our risk. We need to speak frankly with each other—with our lovers, our children, our friends, our young people.

On this day, I will pledge in the future to have safe sex and to become better informed about the transmission of AIDS.

May 30

PATRIOTISM

We are no more aliens to this country or to its institutions than our brothers in white. We have instituted it; our forefathers paid dearly for it. . . . Together we planted the tree of liberty and watered its roots with our tears and blood, and under its branches we will stay and be sheltered.

—THOMAS E. MILLER

Some of us are torn about our patriotism. Can we salute the country that has enslaved us, brutalized us, denied us justice and plain decency? There are those who would raise fists instead.

But when we learn and think about our history here, we are struck by how much our people have done to build and improve this country. Through our struggle and our civil rights victories, we have made America a better place. We have forced our nation to live up to its grand promises of "liberty and justice for all." When we raise the flag, we salute the contributions and the sacrifices of our people.

Today I will take five minutes to meditate upon how African-Americans in general, and my family in particular, have helped build America.

May 31

CHALLENGES

*Someone once told me that God figured that I
was a pretty good juggler. I could keep a lot of
balls in the air at one time. So He said, "Let's
see if you can juggle another one."*

—ARTHUR ASHE

We can easily wail about the indignities, the bad
blows, the bum luck, the unfairness of life—or, we
can accept them all as challenges. With one stance
we allow ourselves to be downtrodden victims. When
bad luck befalls us, we take it as a cue that we should
not expect anything good out of our lives.

When we view our lives as a juggling act or a
sort of sporting contest, we learn to go along with
the limitations and obstacles that are dealt us, and
find ways to make it through the event in good form
and with our energy up. Different talents and
strengths will be called upon to make it through. Our
faith, humor, and optimism may be tested, but they
will keep us going as long as we make the effort to
refuel them.

*On this day, I will take five minutes to remember a
time when I met and succeeded with a challenge.*

STRENGTH

*I've talked to so many who believe they are
supposed to be superhuman and bear up under
all things. When they don't, they all too readily
look for the fault within themselves.*

—GLORIA NAYLOR

We all have a large number of responsibilities and
duties to others and ourselves. If from time to time
we fail, we shouldn't beat ourselves up!

Sure, sometimes we could have done better,
but a lot of times there are situations beyond our
control. We're not superhuman. Let's give ourselves
a break!

*On this day, I will take five minutes to consider and
accept both my strengths and my frailties, and I will
pledge to use my strengths to buttress my frailties.*

June 2

ENCOURAGEMENT

You can't regiment spirit, and
it is the spirit that counts.

—ROMARE BEARDEN

We can rarely expect ourselves and others to fall in line at a command. What we *can* do is encourage, motivate, and allow opportunities for the spirit to flourish. We need to show our children the world's possibilities, giving them the chance to become aware and excited about their own talents and interests. We need to give our loved ones time, space, and emotional support so they can get in touch with their passions. Excitement is contagious; commands are a drag.

On this day, I pledge to encourage and support friends and other African-Americans in their endeavors.

STRUGGLE

We must recognize the awesome demands of time, effort, and life of serious struggle. The struggle is a long and difficult one; therefore we must mask no difficulties, tell no lies and claim no easy victory.

—MAULANA KARENGA

It's true we've made progress. We're no longer enslaved; we have an expanding middle class and more power and representation. Still, we cannot overestimate that power. Look at those who command the nation's top banks, media organizations, and oil industries and you will not see African-American faces. We have a long way to go.

We must also keep in mind that even the progress we've made can be eroded. We have only to look at post-Reconstruction—its lynching, Ku Klux Klan terrorism, and frightening clampdown on our newborn rights as citizens—to be reminded of that.

Our challenges need not demoralize us. We get there one step at a time.

On this day, I will do at least one thing that will advance me toward one of my goals.

ACCEPTANCE/APPRECIATION

*I've accepted my reality. I was meant
to sound the way I do.*

—KATHLEEN BATTLE

"Accepting our reality" can sound like a cop-out, an excuse for not changing or challenging ourselves. But why is our "reality" always perceived as lacking? Perhaps our reality has provided us with some absolutely stunning possibilities.

Knowing ourselves can be a futile exercise if it implies rejecting ourselves. Kathleen Battle's crystalline soprano voice may not be suited to opera's heavier, dramatic roles, but to our good fortune, Ms. Battle chooses to showcase what she has to heartstopping effect.

Sometimes we feel the need to change things about ourselves. Other times, we've just got to acknowledge our reality and run with it.

*On this day, I will take five minutes to take stock of
all my physical and personality traits and will give
thanks for having those traits.*

AFFIRMATIVE ACTION

They have made affirmative action a dirty word.
For us, it's a word that means fairness.

—ULYSSES JONES

Memphis firefighter Jones believes he would not have made lieutenant if a lawsuit brought by African-Americans against the city and the firefighters' union had not forced the department to award 20 percent of its promotions to minorities.

Jones is only one of so many of us who have benefited from affirmative action. But now some of us are questioning the policies that helped us, claiming they stigmatize us and make us suspect, as though we are not up to our jobs.

But what about whites who've received preferential treatment through legacies, where children of alumni are favored over other applicants; and the old-boy-network system of recruiting from within?

We needn't obsess about how we got to where we are. We need only focus on getting the task before us done.

On this day, I will focus on the job before me and do it to the best of my ability.

OPTIMISM

All my life I've had this almost criminal optimism. I didn't care what happened, the glass was always going to be half full.

—QUINCY JONES

Optimism can seem the easiest thing for some. In the face of such overwhelming self-assurance, we begin to wonder about ourselves.

Most of us have our bleaker moments. Our defeats, both big and small, can wind us for a bit. It's how we respond to them that matters—whether we shake them off and get on with business or allow them to sink our dreams.

Optimism can be rehearsed so it becomes a conditioned response. Positive thinking is a habit worth developing. Through it, we remind ourselves that we are talented, hardworking, and worthy of success.

On this day, I will remember a time when I felt down, and I will imagine myself being optimistic—figuring out how to make the momentary setback work in my favor or inspire me to try to do something else.

June 7

IMAGINATION

Nor here, nor there; the roving fancy flies,
Till some lov'd object strikes her wandering eyes.
Whose silken fetters all the senses bind,
And soft captivity involves the mind.

—PHILLIS WHEATLEY

It is a wonderful feeling, indeed, when our mind is captivated by a notion that intrigues us and stirs our creativity. Imagination fuels and motivates us. We must guard against shackling it; our imagination, without free rein, will wither. Set free, it can take us anywhere.

On this day, I will take five minutes to imagine that I have accomplished one of my goals and allow that image to inspire me.

FEAR

Life has frightened me now and then,
and if I've ever shown uncommon bravery,
I've failed to notice it.

—GORDON PARKS

As adults, we try to deny or shunt aside what frightens us because it's not acceptable or easy to admit when we're scared. We will not be cowards. We'll be strong.

Life *can* be frightening. Death, disease, and destitution lurk hidden in the corners. We can spend our lives dodging failure and rejection. We *don't* feel particularly brave; we're too busy just making it through the moment. But we can certainly be alarmed by the feelings of anger, violence, and despair that threaten to well up inside us.

Fear is a signal. When we can identify what frightens us, we can begin to cope with it in a positive way.

On this day, I will take five minutes to make note of
at least one fear I might have, and I will examine
that fear to see if I should really be afraid of it. If so,
I pledge to come up with a way of coping with it.

LOVE

If you're going to be sick and not sure about the future of your life, it's pretty nice to have someone who loves you.

—SAMMY DAVIS, JR.

It's also pretty nice when you're healthy and optimistic about the future to have someone who loves you. That might be a lover or a friend—or a number of friends. When we find people in our lives with whom we can be ourselves, it can be wonderfully gratifying and freeing.

The relationships that last are the ones that are mutually satisfying—we may treasure a friend's sense of humor and spontaneity while he may value our warmth and thoughtfulness. The person who demands too much or expects us to share all his views and interests will stifle our growth and our personality. We must not neglect ourselves in order to maintain or prolong a friendship or romance.

There is great joy in finding that special connection with someone, in enjoying their company and enjoying ourselves when we are with them.

On this day, I will make some small gesture of affection to a special person in my life.

WINNING

The majority of people in the world don't do what it takes to win. Everyone is looking for the easy road.

—CHARLES BARKLEY

What does it take to win? Certainly, the desire to win. Also, commitment to pursue our goals; the ability to focus our energy on our goals; the obstinacy to face hurdles, endure setbacks, and hang in there long after others have given up. Not only must we forge ahead despite the skepticism of others, but we must quash our own self-doubts as they crop up.

None of this is easy. Success does not come when we want it to. It may take years longer than we'd hoped. We have to resist getting sidetracked and disillusioned. We also have to be flexible and improvise.

There may be nothing wrong with taking the easy road, so long as we do not pine for the destination at the end of the difficult road. But it is often the difficult road that provides the most scenic route.

On this day, I pledge to do at least one thing that will advance me toward my goal.

STEREOTYPES

When they approach me they see . . .
everything and anything except me.
— RALPH ELLISON, *from* The Invisible Man

We are invisible to many white people because what they see is not who we are, but some stereotype. On the street, white women pull their handbags closer as African-American men pass. It doesn't matter how we're dressed. While he was a grad student at Harvard University, Cornell West recalls, "The first thing I ever taught was a class on 'Antigone,' in which a student thought I was a janitor and asked me to get more chairs."

These indignities happen to us all the time. We get frustrated and angry. But we cannot waste our energy on others' misconceptions. We cannot afford to let our anger linger and feed on itself so that it prevents us from focusing on our goals and detracts from our happiness.

On this day, I will spend five minutes and focus on
the things that make me unique and good—both
physically and spiritually.

*The Met was the first mountain I climbed
successfully. I had said no to them when I felt
I wasn't ready. When I debuted, I was
technically prepared and highly negotiable. I
was box-office.*

—LEONTYNE PRICE

"Yes" and "no" may well be the trickiest words in
our language. We may have been advised always to
say yes to challenges, especially where career is concerned. We fret that it appears cowardly to say no.
We certainly want to grab at the chances we get,
because who knows when they'll come around again.

It comes down to our instincts, our gut feelings. There are times when saying no is the smartest
thing, and the most courageous thing, too. Saying
no can be a terrific strategy, giving us time to prepare
and develop. We have to monitor ourselves, though.
If we notice that we've made a habit of saying no,
we might be letting fear rather than wisdom rule us.

*Responding too quickly can be our biggest mistake.
On this day, I pledge that I will keep my own needs
in mind before giving an answer.*

WANDERING

I was always the chronic wanderer, taking off on a bus or subway to the end of the line.

—CICELY TYSON

We usually point to those who are fixed on their goals as the ones who will succeed. What about those of us who feel we're wandering? Are we doomed to stay directionless? Not if we're alert.

The focused individual may have her eyes so trained on the path ahead that she never glances to the side to see if there's a more promising route. When we occasionally wander, we may actually notice more possibilities for our lives.

This is not to advocate chucking our specific goals or throwing ourselves off course, only to suggest we can benefit by being flexible.

On this day, I pledge to spend five minutes visualizing myself remaining flexible and being aware of interesting opportunities that come along the way.

SELF-DELUSION

When face-to-face with one's self . . . there is no cop-out.

—*EDWARD KENNEDY "DUKE" ELLINGTON*

With others, we can pretend. We wear our masks, adopt an attitude; we can even lie through our teeth. When we look in the mirror, the mask evaporates and we see the truth.

We owe it to ourselves not to be deluded, but to accept ourselves, warts and all. Seeing the warts, knowing they're there, can be part of our growth process.

It shouldn't require five years in analysis to learn the truth about ourselves. Look daily in the mirror, and make sure the reflection is clear.

On this day, I will take five minutes to look at something in my behavior or attitude that might be stopping me from reaching one of my goals. Then I will determine how I can address the problem even if only for today.

June 15

FAITH

Quit talking about dying; if you believe your
God is all-powerful, believe He is powerful
enough to open these prison doors. . . . Pray to
live and believe you are going to get out.

—IDA B. WELLS

Ida B. Wells's quote refers to a visit she made to a Little Rock, Arkansas, jail where twelve African-American men who had been unjustly accused were awaiting electrocution. Wells listened as the men prayed about dying and being welcomed into heaven because they were innocent. She bade them pray in a more positive manner. A concerted drive by African-Americans culminated successfully in the men's release.

Prayer can be one of our most powerful methods of positive thinking—if we pose our prayers in the right way. Let's ask for God's power to guide us toward victory.

On this day, I will take five minutes to reflect upon
what gives my life meaning. I will use a song, line of
poetry, or comforting image from my past to help
renew my strength when I am in despair or when I
need inspiration to go on fighting.

CHILDREN

*Black people know how to save our children.
Our little children are the most intuitive, the
brightest kids. To reach them we just have to
get back to basics.*

—NELLIE COOKE

Child-rearing can be frightening to the best-prepared
and most eager parent. We will likely meet with success when we allow ourselves to be guided by both
our intellect and compassion. Our children must feel
secure in their environment, loved and respected and
proud. At the same time, we must be clear about
what is unacceptable behavior; when we discipline
with love instead of anger or abuse, our children will
be able to retain their dignity even when they see
they have erred. We can help to instill in them pride
and a can-do attitude that they will carry though
life's adversities.

*On this day, I will spend time with a child or
children; I will take a few minutes to let them know
that I appreciate their unique talents.*

MEDIA IMAGES

The revolution will not be televised.
—*GIL SCOTT HERON*

The revolution African-Americans are part of is the one we wage to empower ourselves and strengthen our people. Generally, it is a quiet one, not afforded great amounts of recognition by the media, who seem fixed more often on our pathologies than on our progress.

When we contemplate the images we see of ourselves on television, we need to remember that what we see is not the whole picture and is not a full representation of who we are.

Let us not look to the media to validate our efforts. Let's look to ourselves.

On this day, I will do at least one concrete thing that will advance me toward my goal.

June 18

BELIEF

Those who believe in ghosts always see them.
                                    —CHARLES V. ROMAN

Substitute for "ghosts" hope, progress, success, or whatever word you choose, and you get the idea.

When we believe that there are good and positive things in life, we will find them. When we think pessimistically, we are also going to find a lot in life to support our view.

Allowing, or even forcing, ourselves to be positive thinkers ensures we will not become mired in the swamp of negativism.

Cynicism is easy, but it promises self-defeat. Claiming that we are being "realistic" by being negative can be immobilizing; we focus on life's difficulties and ignore its possibilities.

Let us believe in ourselves and our visions of self-fulfillment so we can begin to attain them.

At the end of this day, I will look for at least one good thing that has happened to me.

COURAGE

*I became more courageous by doing the very
things I needed to be courageous for—first, a
little, and badly. Then, bit by bit, more and
better. Being avidly—sometimes annoyingly—
curious and persistent about discovering how
others were doing what I wanted to do.*

—AUDRE LORDE

In all of us there is the aptitude for courage. We are
courageous when we dare to grow, to change, to accomplish, to fulfill our dreams for ourselves or strive
to enable our children to fulfill theirs. We are gutsy
when we risk failing, when we try new things, when
we squeeze our way into places to see what it is we
need to learn and do. We are brave when we are
persistent and undeterred by setbacks.

Courage allows us to be ourselves and to accept
ourselves.

*On this day, I will take five minutes to remember a
time I risked failing, asked a question that seemed
foolish, was persistent in a request . . . and was
rewarded.*

COMPASSION

Judge not the brother! There are secrets in his heart that you might weep to see.

—EGBERT MARTIN

There are few people we ever come to know with great intimacy. Even our spouses and lovers may be reluctant to share the hurts and fears and anguish in their hearts with us. We usually act with only partial knowledge of a person, and generally it is our own feelings we focus on.

We need not make elaborate excuses for all those who wrong us throughout our lives. We cannot allow ourselves to become abused. But generosity of spirit can salvage worthwhile and meaningful relationships. We can offer our ears and our understanding, but we cannot press another to open up what he prefers to keep closed.

When we understand how our own experiences have shaped us, we can begin to show compassion to others who may not have been so fortunate.

On this day, I will remember a time in which I was compassionate or forgiving.

STRENGTH

They'll never count me among the broken men.
                    —GEORGE LESTER JOHNSON

Sheer obstinacy can sometimes be our greatest weapon. When we talk about hanging tough, we dare the world to break us. The magic lies within us, in our will to overcome all the adversity flung our way, to refuse to accept degradation. But what is it that puts one person and not another on the street when times get tough? Could it happen to us?

Some are indeed stronger than others. Perhaps they have triumphed over despair already and have come out of it more confident. It seems that if you learn to value *yourself*—not your money or your earning potential or your possessions—and carry that faith and belief in your heart, mind, and soul, nothing in the world can break you.

On this day I will take five minutes to consider the experiences in my life that have strengthened me, and I will allow myself to feel strong and capable and undeterred in pursuing my goals.

QUESTIONING

*O my body, make of me always a man
who questions.*

—FRANTZ FANON

If we fail to question, whose answers are we accepting
as the truth? Blind trust can be lethal. Clinging to
the views we adopted years ago can mean we are
afraid to find we may need to change.

We worry that examining our behavior and our
motivations can make us appear insecure or timid.
Sometimes we take lifelong stands that cripple or
pain us, but still we are adamant about our positions
and too proud to rethink them. Our notions about
being masculine, feminine, old, or black can work
against us, but do we challenge them?

Questioning—ourselves and others—can be
the bravest way to live our lives.

*On this day, I will think of at least one thing I take
for granted. I will take five minutes to ask myself why
I do it that way, and I will come up with at least one
other way to do it.*

June 23

ACTIVISM

If you have a microphone, you have a responsibility to make your opinions known.
—JOHN SINGLETON

A film director has the ability to project his vision of the world, to make a statement or pose a question, to help us see things more clearly or in a different light. But what can *we* do to make our opinions known? Most of us don't feel we have the microphone; we don't want to look like hollering fools, either.

There *are* ways to be heard, to get across the things we view as important. The idea is to be alert and active. If an issue in our community concerns us, we can write letters to the newspaper, call the mayor's office, sign petitions, go to town meetings, join tenant or neighborhood associations. We all have access to microphones; we all should make our opinions known.

My voice is important, and I pledge to make it heard today.

POWER

Power concedes nothing without demand; it never has and it never will.

—FREDERICK DOUGLASS

It is often implied, if not squarely put, that African-Americans should be grateful for any goodies we get in this country—whether we're talking about a promotion at work or moving into a certain apartment building or section of town. What we have to remember is that we *deserve* whatever good we get and that we need not bend over backward to thank people who merely treated us fairly.

Sometimes when we land a job or promotion, we'll be told how lucky we are. We will be expected to fill a chair while the full rights and powers of the position are withheld. We have to *demand* those rights so that we have the power we need to function. And we must be prepared to demand, struggle, and fight for them.

On this day, I will do at least one concrete thing that will take me closer to one of my goals.

SILENCE

If you're silent for a long time,
people just arrive in your mind.

—ALICE WALKER

The "people" Alice Walker refers to are the characters in her stories.

When we are quiet and relaxed, ideas come to us. It may take some doing to let the stress and aggravations of daily life go, but if we can give ourselves that time, we may find ways to cut down on that stress. Life will then become more meaningful and pleasurable.

On this day, I will take five minutes to be silent and listen to my thoughts and observe my mental images as they float by my mind's eye.

June 26

ENVIRONMENTALISM

Treat the world well. . . . It was not given to you by your parents. . . . It was lent to you by your children.

—*Kenyan proverb*

We look around to find our world in terrible shape—rivers and oceans polluted, holes in the ozone layer, garbage dumped into our Earth that won't break down for thousands of years. And while we may not personally feel the blame, it is up to all mankind to save our planet for our grandchildren and their grandchildren.

Let us remember our ancestors and their feeling of harmony with the land and with nature. That is in us, too; let's tap into it so that our lives are more beautiful and less toxic.

On this day, I pledge always to throw away my trash. And I pledge today to put in a trash can at least one wrapper or piece of trash that I am not responsible for.

PRIDE

*I haunted the city dumps and the trash piles
behind hotels, retrieving discarded linen and
kitchenware . . . broken chairs. . . . Everything
was scoured and mended. This was part of the
training to salvage, to reconstruct, to make
bricks without straw.*

—MARY MCLEOD BETHUNE

In starting up her school for African-American children in 1904, Mary McLeod Bethune found a way
to "make bricks without straw." She succeeded in
her goal because she was not too proud to scavenge
dumps and scrub the throwaways of others. Indeed,
it was her pride in herself and her personal mission
that revealed resources where others might have seen
none.

Let's not permit our sense of "dignity" to rob
us of our chances. Others may shake their heads,
but we will persevere and gather our rewards.

*On this day, I will take five minutes to note all I am
proud of, and I will remember that I am also secure
enough to do what needs to be done to accomplish one
of my goals.*

SEX

There are some of us who are just too grateful to be loved, and this applies to men as well as women. Women who regard men as bank accounts are as wrongheaded as men who treat women as either trophies or housekeepers. We need to see through to the individuals our partners are. And we must hold to our dignity and make sure that we communicate our needs and feelings. With mutual respect we will know the privilege of love and live up to it.

On this day, I pledge to reaffirm my self-worth and let no one treat me with disrespect. I will also acknowledge that those I love or may yet fall in love with are to be treated as I would wish to be treated.

June 29

HOME

*Don't you realize that the sea is the home of
the water? All water is off on a journey
unlessen it's in the sea, and it's homesick, and
bound to make its way home someday.*

—ZORA NEALE HURSTON,
from Seraph on the Suwanee

▶▮▮▮▮◀▶▮▮▮▮◀

Few of us would deny the importance of home. Our home can bring us a sense of beauty, peace, and safety in a difficult world. There can be great satisfaction in creating a pleasing environment. It might be the shape of an inexpensive vase or the grouping of old family photos that touches us.

Our homes must contain an atmosphere that is conducive to reading, thinking, and studying, and this is especially vital with children in the home.

*On this day, I will do at least one thing to beautify
my home. For example, I might put a drawer in
order, clean a room, or put a vase of flowers or a bowl
of fresh fruit on the table.*

CHANGE

Each time I sing, it's a new experience for me. None of the roles I have done has yet reached a pinnacle: They are always evolving and being reevaluated.

—KATHLEEN BATTLE

How often do we lament that life is just more of the same old stuff? We needn't accept monotony or boredom as a permanent factor in our lives. For instance, each time we serve dinner, it need not be the same as every dinner that went before. We can vary the menu, use different plates or napkins, put different flowers on the table. Every Saturday night we spend with our spouse or longtime companion, we need not lapse into a routine we find stultifying. We are all creative, and as long as we are willing to take the initiative, we can find ways to invigorate our lives and our relationships.

On this day, no matter how content I may be with my routine, I will try something new, whether it means substituting tea for coffee or taking a new route to work or picking up a new magazine or newspaper.

UNFAIRNESS/CHALLENGES

*She informed us regularly and matter-of-factly
that we had to be twice as good as white
children in everything we attempted in life.
"That way you got half a chance of making it."*
—BEBE MOORE CAMPBELL, *from* Sweet Summer

Who among us has not heard this bit of wisdom?
We may hate the unfairness behind it, the prejudice
that accounts for its validity, but can we ignore it?
Not if we aspire to making it. On the other hand,
"making it" can be a highly subjective matter. For
some, "making it" implies amassing wealth and living high on the hog. But if, in doing so, we frustrate
our true impulses and fail to find fulfillment, we have
not "made it," but lost it.

Racism, classism, sexism, homophobia, and
ageism are challenges. When we force ourselves to
work twice as hard as others, however, the rewards
are *ours* to enjoy. We and future generations are the
beneficiaries. The important thing is to be working
at something we find meaningful and worthwhile.

*On this day, I will do at least one concrete thing that
advances me toward one of my goals.*

FULFILLMENT

The human heart is a strange mystery.
—ALEXANDRE DUMAS, FILS

Yes, the heart can be fickle, or cold or soft, or empty. It can beat with passion, clutch with emotion, and stop in awe or terror. We are often surprised by the unpredictability of our hearts. If we have distanced ourselves from our emotions, we can be shocked by the swiftness and intensity of our feelings.

There will always be mystery in the workings of our hearts, but we can get to know and understand ourselves better if we are in touch with our feelings and the things that drive and motivate us. What can we hope to gain by such self-analysis? We can enrich our lives when we discover what makes our heart race, what makes it tick with contentment and beat with purpose.

On this day, I will take five minutes to think about what I want to do with my life. Do I feel productive? Fulfilled? What can I do that will increase my sense of satisfaction and accomplishment?

July 3

PATRIOTISM

*I feel that I am a citizen of the American
dream, that the revolutionary struggle of which
I am a part is a struggle against the American
nightmare.*

—ELDRIDGE CLEAVER

Think about it: Anything we African-Americans do
to progress is revolutionary because we are tilting the
balance of power. Everything we do that speaks to
African-American empowerment and pride is a revolutionary statement in this society which has
historically rejected it.

Knowledge of ourselves and our heritage gives
us the courage to assume our rightful, equal role
here. When we take or demand full participation, we
live out what our country promises all its citizens—
the American dream.

*On this day, I will take five minutes to meditate
upon how African-Americans in general, and my
family in particular, have helped build America.*

July 4

ADVERSITY

In every adversity, look for the benefit that can come out of it. Even bad experiences offer benefits; but you have to look for them.

—JOHN E. COPAGE

Usually, when we've gotten through a bad experience, we just want to put it behind us and move on. We don't want to linger over the guilt or pain, and with good reason. Who wants to dwell forever on past mistakes or hurts?

Still, if we refuse to look critically at the experience, we cannot hope to learn or benefit by it. Perhaps we have discovered something of our strength, or conversely, we have been alerted to our fragility.

On this day, I will take five minutes to remember a time when I was confronted with adversity and imagine how I can use the situation to become a stronger person.

POWER

Successful black men seem instinctively to understand something of the nature of power— that while it may be denied, it can also be assumed, claimed, seized, and exercised, for it is neither finite nor ordained.

—AUDREY EDWARDS and CRAIG K. POLITE, from Children of the Dream

Sometimes we—men and women—fall into the trap of thinking that power is beyond our reach. But we are not at the absolute mercy of others. We can do our jobs so well that power cannot be denied us. We can make ourselves so indispensable and visible that we, in a sense, create our own power. When we are frustrated, however, we must be willing to leave; to go somewhere that has more room for our ambition.

There are many who would deny us power; let's not do it to ourselves.

On this day, I will visualize one of my goals and acknowledge that it is within my reach.

July 6

UNIQUENESS

*For a long time, I thought I was ugly and
disfigured. This made me shy and timid, and I
often reacted to insults that were not intended.
. . . I believe, though, that it was from this
period . . . that I really began to see people and
things.*

—ALICE WALKER

It can be hard for us to shake our old self-images,
even if we have lost the pounds that imprisoned us,
or straightened the teeth that kept us from smiling.
When we feel that we stand out in some unpleasant
way, we often distance ourselves rather than face rejection and humiliation.

Mercifully, other people will not always suffer
from our own hard self-assessment and can challenge
us to see the good and special qualities we possess.

*On this day, I will take five minutes to think about
ways in which I am different from other people, and I
will think about how I can or do use those differences
to help me accomplish one of my goals.*

APPRECIATION

*I'll pick up little books or cards and send them
to [my son] with a message that may simply
say, "You're a wonderful son."*

—NATALIE COLE

We all need reinforcement. Small gestures can have
a powerful cumulative effect. They can positively reinforce a child's self-image, strengthen a romantic
relationship, and help us maintain a lifelong
friendship.

Let's let our parents, children, friends, lovers,
spouses know how wonderful they are. Let it be our
voices that speak and not some greeting-card man-
ufacturer's. Showing our appreciation puts us into a
brighter mood and lets us know how blessed we are.
What a healthy and affirmative habit! When we are
in the practice of acknowledging the good in life, our
motivation is strengthened and our spirits uplifted.

*On this day, I will call or send a small gift or write a
brief note of affection to my mate, child, parent, loved
one, or friend.*

July 8

ACTION

When the snake is in the house,
one need not discuss the matter at length.
— *EWE proverb*

We sometimes talk a matter to death. We revel in our powers of observation and analysis, our astuteness in assessing the situation, and our psychological insights into its cause. What we really need is action, because talking out a thing is not the same as fixing it.

African-Americans are by now well versed in our problems and the causes that brought them about—from slavery to current racism. Many of our brothers and sisters feel frustrated and oppressed. Will mere talk or sermonizing put an end to our dilemmas?

We must focus more on solving the problems, turning our insights into action. This goes for *all* our difficulties, personal as well as communal. There is a time for talk . . . . and a time for action.

On this day, I will do one thing that brings me
nearer to accomplishing one of my goals.

July 9

FAITH

My relationship with God has helped me avoid
problems others have run into.

—BARRY SANDERS

Most of us believe in a higher power, whether God,
Allah, or a guiding spirit within. Faith in that higher
power can help us to make the right decisions in our
lives. Sometimes we stumble, but if we have faith,
we can believe that things will work out for the best.

Even when adversity hits us, faith can buoy us
up and carry us along to something better. We are
born to succeed and flourish, to do our best, to make
the right choices, and to reflect the goodness that is
divine.

On this day, I will take five minutes to remember
that God (or the guiding spirit within me) wants me
to succeed in my endeavors, and is at all times
making opportunities available to me to help me in
my life.

SUPPORT

*I could draw a circle on a piece of paper and
my mother made me feel like Van Gogh.*
—DAMON WAYANS

When we have been raised in a supportive environment, we start life with a leg up. But what do we do if we either did not receive that reinforcement in our youth or have not yet found a way to stand on our own?

It's up to us to make ourselves feel good, strong, valuable, significant. We must find the "stuff" inside us that makes us feel proud, and we must make sure that we surround ourselves with people who support and affirm us. We must let our friends and mates know that, for our own health, we will not tolerate their negative tunes. When we show support, we will often get support in return, but if we don't, we must communicate our needs.

*On this day, I will take five minutes to make a list of
some of my good traits, strengths, and abilities.*

POWER

*Power doesn't mean you're acting like a man,
or you're a bully or a bitch. It's that you don't
let people step on you.*

—SHARON MONPLAISIR

World-class fencer Sharon Monplaisir knows about
power. And she doesn't worry that her athletic ability
negates her femininity.

It's odd the way we come up with notions of
what's acceptable based on gender. To be feminine
doesn't mean we have to lose our power; to be masculine doesn't mean we have to abuse it.

True power has nothing to do with the little
games we play with each other. When we know our
self-worth and demand the respect we deserve, our
power works for us.

*On this day, I will close my eyes and feel my power.
I will see myself in control and handling every
situation calmly and efficiently.*

AGE

There ain't nothin' an ol' man can do but bring
me a message from a young one.

— JACKIE "MOMS" MABLEY

Our society devalues older people. Most of us thank the Lord we're not old, which, depending on our age, can be anywhere from thirty to ninety. Youth has come to represent vitality, creativity, and accomplishment. And while age implies wisdom and earns respect in some places, it seems to suggest to us inactivity, deterioration, and an intellectual and creative drying up.

We must not let any number of years have power over us. Every day of our lives has the potential to enrich us and to see growth. Look around. There are so many older people who are vital and creative. Their contributions are important. Let's be inspired by them. They have seen much, endured much, and still they have dreams.

On this day, I will do something thoughtful for an
elder. Or if I feel bad about aging, I will plan to do
something self-affirming.

July 13

INDEPENDENCE

*People thought they had to protect me from a
lot of things. In doing so, they denied me a
chance to grow, to experience the things that
give a person a certain amount of growth and
maturity. I've had to make up for all that lost
time in recent years, but I don't blame anyone.*

—KAREEM ABDUL-JABBAR

We can thank our friends for their concern—we can
take their advice to heart—but ultimately we must
steer our own way past life's potential pits and dan-
gers. If we're going to make mistakes, let them be
our own. We cannot hope to learn and grow when
we shirk our responsibility to ourselves.

*On this day, I will take five minutes to reevaluate the
direction of my life. If I am not satisfied, I will map
out a course of action to change it.*

July 14

COLLECTIVE WORK/
COLLECTIVE RESPONSIBILITY

*Injustice doesn't have to occur to me personally,
but I react personally and I am compelled to do
something about it.*

—ROSE SANDERS

We've heard the news reports about conditions in
South Africa and the unconscionable Rodney King
verdict and the rage rises inside us. Can we help, and
how? Just what are we morally bound to do?

We alone can determine what our capabilities
are, but we must realize we *can* make a difference.
We can write letters to newspapers and magazines,
march, become informed voters, spend our money in
our community, and, if we are so inclined, donate
time, money, or expertise to those less fortunate.

*On this day, I will do something to help or give
encouragement to my fellow African-Americans.*

July 15

PERSEVERANCE/WILL

*Life is like a slot machine. The coins you put
into it are work and ideas. And, unlike a Las
Vegas slot machine, you can influence the
chances of winning with your will.*

—BESSIE COPAGE

In Las Vegas and Atlantic City casinos, people will
feed dollar after dollar into the slot machines in the
hope that the next coin will pay off big. When it
comes to accomplishing something in their lives,
they will make a stab or two and give up.

We've got to keep trying till all the cherries
line up: the right idea at the right place at the right
time. It could take lots of coins (work and ideas), but
someone eventually wins. Why not us?

*On this day, I will do one thing that will take me one
step closer to one of my goals.*

July 16

SELF-LOVE

*Long tresses down to the floor can be beautiful,
if you have that, but learn to love what you
have.*

—ANITA BAKER

How often do we smile when we look in the mirror?
Frequently we're too busy focusing on the "flaws" we
find.

What a shame we don't learn to love ourselves
the way we are. We talk about our "imperfections,"
thereby assuming that there is such a thing as a "perfect" beauty.

Sad to say, some African-Americans are still
allowing themselves to be guided by European notions of beauty. We can't lose sleep over the hang-
ups of our brothers and sisters, but we can learn to
compliment ourselves when we look in the mirror.
With practice, it becomes automatic.

*On this day, I will spend five minutes and focus on
the good things about myself—physically and
spiritually.*

July 17

WISDOM

*At twenty-two, I thought I knew everything.
Now, at sixty-seven, I find I haven't tasted a
drop from the sea of knowledge. The more I
learn, the more I find out how little I know.*
—JOHN E. COPAGE

Sad to say, a number of us stop learning with any
ferocity at an early age. It may actually be despite
our best intentions that the door to our mind closes.
The demands of earning a living, of raising a family,
and of contributing to the community in which we
live crowd our lives, leaving little time for nourishing
our minds. We dole out our hours this way and that,
perhaps allocating time for physical exercise, time for
relaxation with friends and family, but no time to
feed our intellectual hunger outside of the odd museum visit or public-television show.

The ocean of knowledge is vast; we need to dip
into it as often as we can for enrichment and our
personal cultivation.

*On this day, I will read the front page of the
newspaper, read a magazine or a chapter from a
book, or have a conversation with somebody—really
listen to him or her and ask questions.*

FIGHTING

I got into very few fights when I played for the Celtics, but every single one of them was in the last quarter, after the game was decided. You have to choose when to fight.

—BILL RUSSELL

There will be times when we have to fight. We can be smart about it and select the time that is advantageous to us, or we can allow ourselves to be driven by the heat of the moment. Even the school bully knows enough not to strike when the principal is watching.

On this day, I will take five minutes to remember various times when I had to decide how to handle conflict. If I handled it appropriately, I will meditate on that. If I feel I should have handled it differently, I will imagine that I am doing so, and meditate on all the good that will come from that.

July 19

RESILIENCY

I still dream big at times, but when my dreams pull apart, as they sometimes do, I don't press the panic button.

—GORDON PARKS

Knowing how to recover when a dream "pulls apart" can make the difference between conquering defeat or being conquered by it.

When we are in a creative mode, a number of ideas come to mind in addition to the ones on which we choose to focus. It helps to keep track of these ideas so that we can draw upon them later. When we have done all we can to realize our current dream, we can get to work on one of these ideas. Any idea can be a dream; many dreams can be made to come true.

On this day, I will take five minutes to remember how strong and resilient I am, and that although I may have gone through difficult times, I am still striving to accomplish my goals.

July 20

HOPE

We never lost hope despite the segregated world of this rural town because we had adults who gave us a sense of a future—and black folk had an extra lot of problems, and we were taught that we could struggle and change them.

—MARIAN WRIGHT EDELMAN

There are many of us brimming with hope and anticipation for the future, yet there are too many more who have given up.

It may take daily positive thinking to convince ourselves that we, individually, are special, gifted, deserving people. We can personally inspire others by exorcising our demons—our cynicism, our destructive habits—and by acknowledging the value inside our hearts and heads, and putting it to use.

On this day, I will pledge to affirm my individual and African-American communal power to continue to seize and create opportunities for a better life.

July 21

READING/EDUCATION

If I was not reading in the [prison] library, I was reading on my bunk. You couldn't have gotten me out of books with a wedge.

—MALCOLM X

◆〉||||||〈◆〉||||||〈◆

We have our busy lives and many demands upon our time and energy. Besides, what can reading do to help us in our mission to strengthen and empower ourselves?

Reading does not detract from our focus but simultaneously helps to broaden and clarify it. We can search out nonfiction books that reflect our experience as African-Americans, that offer nutrition advice or child-rearing information. Novels can feed our souls.

As each of us discovers the power of reading, our African-American community is strengthened immeasurably.

On this day, I will read the front page of the newspaper, read a magazine, or read a chapter from a book.

July 22

GUILT

Not much is going to come from another guilt trip for white America.

—WYATT TEE WALKER

Let's get this straight. America owes us and owes us big—for the blood we shed on battlefields fighting for other people's liberty while denied our own, and for the sweat spilled on the farmlands and in the factories across America to put money in the pockets of others while our children went shoeless and malnourished, or, worse, were sold.

We have not been given reparations for past injustices done us, unlike some other groups. We should keep in mind and press for what is owed us, but we cannot make this the sole focus of our attention. Guilt over the past has never, by itself, resulted in restitution for African-Americans.

On this day, I will take five minutes to think about the sacrifices African-Americans have made for the United States. And I will let my feelings about those sacrifices fuel me to do at least one thing that advances me toward one of my goals today.

July 23

DIGNITY

No race can prosper till it learns that there is as much dignity in tilling a field as in writing a poem.

—BOOKER T. WASHINGTON

We often devalue those who cannot validate their existence in terms of money and power. We cluck with pride when our daughter proclaims her intention of becoming a doctor or lawyer. But is it written in any job description that the pay is $70,000 a year, plus dignity dividends?

Dignity is a thing unattached to a job title, an address, or a fancy car. All of us have known many people with great dignity who didn't have a fancy job, house, or car. Such people know that self-worth has nothing to do with material goods or others' opinions.

On this day, I will take five minutes to feel the dignity within me and to acknowledge that it is not related to my checkbook or address.

APPROPRIATENESS

*Eating when you are hungry and sleeping when
you are sleepy. That is the ultimate wisdom.*

—BESSIE COPAGE

We can allow ourselves to feel angry, but then we
need to get on with life. Just as we eat when we're
hungry and stop (ideally) when we're full, we can experience our emotions and then move on. We don't
need to feel guilty about our reactions and shouldn't
feel we have to change them unless we find that they
are destructive to ourselves or others.

*I trust myself to respond in an appropriate and life-
affirming way to any situation. On this day, I will
take five minutes to remember a time when I acted
spontaneously and everything worked out well.*

July 25

ASSISTANCE

*My mind is overtaxed. Brave and courageous
as I am, I feel that creeping on of that
inevitable thing, a breakdown, if I cannot get
some immediate relief. I need somebody to come
and get me.*

—MARY MCLEOD BETHUNE

When we take too much upon our shoulders, it's
almost inevitable that we are going to "break down"
under the weight. We have to learn to ask for the
help we need. There are always sympathetic ears to
be found, ranging from family, friends, and clergy to
city clinics, private professionals, twelve-step programs such as Alcoholics Anonymous, or telephone
crisis lines.

Of course, the help we need may not warrant
the heavy artillery. Still, it's best to act early, when
the problem is manageable.

*On this day, I will remember that there is no shame
in asking for help. I will remember that in accepting
help, I am ultimately helping myself.*

July 26

TOLERANCE

A person is a person because he recognizes others as persons.

—DESMOND TUTU

Yes, even we who should know better are sometimes guilty of dehumanizing others because they do not conform to our code of ethics, because they don't belong to our gang, our gender, our socioeconomic group, or our sexual preference. We start to see others less as persons and reach into our roster of brands: sellouts, bitches, fags, Toms, and losers.

We African-Americans know what it feels like to be dehumanized; we view those who do this to us as less than human. Let's make sure we apply this judgment to ourselves as well, whether we are looking at our more successful, or less fortunate, brothers and sisters, or at those who've made choices we do not understand.

On this day, I will take five minutes to reflect upon the varied nature of black people, our many styles and contributions.

July 27

APPEARANCE

*People should start dressing for success before
they're successful—not after!*

—WILLI SMITH

The way we present ourselves to the world has an
impact. If we are sloppily attired in trousers that
don't fit, a rumpled shirt, and stained tie, we'll make
an impression, all right—one that we will have to
overcome.

We may have to substitute a cotton blouse on
sale for the silk one we'd like· that's fine. Neatness
counts, as do good grooming, a wardrobe appropriate
for the job, and a general "polish."

Let's dress to please and promote ourselves.

*On this day, I'll take an extra few minutes to look in
the mirror and determine if the message I'm projecting
is one that I am proud of and that I feel to be me. If
not, I will take one concrete action—iron my blouse,
change my tie—so that I do feel I am projecting who
I am and what I feel.*

July 28

CHILDREN

We think that our children are ours, but they are only our seed. Their reason and purpose has something to do with them, and I don't think we can take credit for that or try to control it.

—DON CHERRY

When we were children, we often had to battle for our independence and individuality. We should remember what it's like to want to develop ourselves free of parental or other outside influence.

Our desire to protect and fortify our children is admirable, but there comes a point where we've got to accept and love them for all their wonderful quirkiness! We may see a bit of ourselves, our spouse, or our parents in them, but the total person is one we've never known before.

On this day, I will take time to be with a younger loved one—a son or daughter, cousin, grandchild— and let them know that I feel that they have special qualities, and that I love, admire, respect, and cherish those special qualities.

JEALOUSY

Rivalry is better than envy.
—*MONGO proverb*

When we envy, we are spending some of our mind's leisure time on a worthless pursuit. Envy doesn't produce much besides self-pity and a useless lust for the things other people have.

If we envy a friend's new job, we stagnate. Instead, let's update our résumé and figure out our next step. If someone we know loses twenty pounds and that's what we need to do, let's assume that if she can do it, so can we.

On this day, I will do one thing to bring me a step further toward the completion of one of my goals.

July 30

RESPONSIBILITY

*It is quite easy to shout slogans, to sign
manifestos, but it is quite a different matter to
build, manage, command, spend days and
nights seeking the solution of problems.*

—PATRICE LUMUMBA

It doesn't take much energy or commitment to wear
a button or a T-shirt, to shout a slogan, or even to
march for an hour or two. The real work is in the
daily "grind" of working toward our personal and political goals, of managing our lives and careers and
families, of contributing to our communities. And
while our efforts can feel somewhat solitary, it is this
daily work that produces the results we are all after.

Let's learn to appreciate each other for everything we do every day. We have to sustain our joint
energy and commitment. A public statement is nothing without the private effort to back it up.

*On this day, I will take five minutes to look at
something speaking to my pride in my heritage—my
"X" cap, my family photos, African cloth—and let
its lingering mental image inspire me to excellence.*

July 31

ACCEPTANCE

*The only thing you have to be that's important
in life . . . is just go on being your own normal,
black, beautiful selves as women, as human
beings.*

—FANNIE LOU HAMER

Let's include men in this important bit of wisdom.

Perhaps we haven't been feeling too good
about our own normal black self. Maybe we failed to
glimpse the beauty when we peeked. Our current
concerns may have tricked us into thinking that we
were somehow defective. We can spend a lot of time
chastising ourselves for our shortcomings. When did
we become such perfectionists?

It would be smarter and certainly kinder to acknowledge our beings as works in progress. Realizing
we have things to work through should not diminish
our overall appreciation of the self we have experienced these many years.

*On this day, I pledge neither to shy away from
growth in myself, nor to require perfection in order to
like myself. I will recognize through self-love that I am
in a continual state of renewal and evolution.*

CONFIDENCE

*My mother convinced me to learn to enjoy
having people tell me I can't do something.
Now it's second nature; I love to prove people
wrong.*

—ANDRE WARE

People told Andre Ware he couldn't play football.
That was before he won the Heisman trophy.

Why on earth do we tell people they can't do
things? Perhaps because we tell *ourselves* there are
things *we* can't do. We feel threatened by their
ambitions when we have stifled and stomped on
our own.

How can we deal with people who want to limit
or destroy our dreams? We can consider their pessimism a challenge and take special pleasure when we
prove them wrong.

When someone tells us, "You can't," let's
make sure we respond, in our hearts and heads, "I
can."

*On this day, I will take five minutes to remember a
time when someone told me I couldn't do
something—and I proved them wrong.*

EXCELLENCE

Whatever you do, do with all your might.
—AESOP, from "The Boy and the Nettles"

Yes, we all have limited time and energy. Sometimes it's tempting to look for shortcuts, or to give up when things get too hard. But going halfway never yields much satisfaction—it just makes us angry that we "wasted" our time, and whittles away at our self-confidence when we fail.

This applies to everything we do. For example, being a parent "with all your might" could mean taking the time to go to the library with your daughter, inquiring about every school in your area, throwing a ball in the park with your kids, reading a story night after night—and letting your son help make the pancakes even though you can do it twice as fast yourself. The rewards are certainly greater than they could ever be when you simply park your kid in front of the television.

On this day, I will choose a project I have not devoted my entire attention to, and attend to it.

August 3

FRESH STARTS

Facing the rising sun of our new day begun,
Let us march on till victory is won.

—JAMES WELDON JOHNSON

How sad that we rarely allow ourselves truly new days, just a reprise of our old days.

Self-examination is the key to a fresh start. In our march toward personal and collective victory, it is imperative to check our route on the map of our life. Do we need to change direction? Are we prepared to face the terrain that lies ahead? We may well be carrying some burdensome load that keeps us from maintaining the pace we require to reach our goal. We may need to cast off some of the weight that impedes our progress. Let's take a look!

On this day, I will take five minutes to reevaluate the direction of my life. If I am not satisfied, I will map out a course of action to change it.

August 4

ENTHUSIASM

If a man is called to be a street sweeper, he should sweep streets even as Michelangelo painted or Beethoven composed music or Shakespeare wrote poetry.

—MARTIN LUTHER KING, JR.

If only we could capture enthusiasm and sell it by the jar! It's easy for us to understand how some are brimming over with enthusiasm—they're doing what they want to be doing, and are recognized and rewarded for their efforts. Mastery has rewards in itself and contributes to our enthusiasm. And there is no job that can't be performed artfully.

On this day, I will take five minutes and pledge to do everything the best I can.

August 5

MOTIVATION

*It's been said that no one can really motivate
anyone else; all you can do is instill a positive
attitude and hope it catches on.*

—EDDIE ROBINSON

We cannot blame anyone else if we do not feel motivated; motivation comes from within. "Mere" motivation has made millionaires of the most profoundly "disadvantaged" folk whose most significant advantage lay in their positive attitude. We don't all need or want to be millionaires, but we can all be successful at what we choose when we consider our passions and talents, then figure out a way to live by them.

*On this day, I will do at least one thing that
advances me toward one of my goals.*

August 6

SELF-DISCOVERY

There is a complexity about human life that
this society does not supply. From the time
you're born it makes you decide what you're
going to be and where you're going to stand
and are you this or are you that.

—BERNICE JOHNSON REAGON

We learn to respect those who seem focused and sure
of the direction of their lives. Perhaps it's because
we haven't really figured out who *we* are and what *we*
want. Is that so terrible?

Some confusion is perfectly normal from time
to time—life presents us with lots of options, and
self-discovery is a continuing process. Confusion becomes a problem only when it prevents us from
setting off in *any* direction, or settling into any one
course long enough to give ourselves a chance.

On this day, I will take five minutes to be quiet,
listen to my inner self, and determine who I am and
who I want to be.

August 7

PRIVATE THOUGHTS

Blessed is the man who to himself has kept
The high creations of his soul;
Who from his friends as from the grave,
Expected nothing of esteem!
— ALEKSANDR SERGEYEVICH PUSHKIN

Many of us—perhaps most—want to be recognized for our achievements, our insights, our contributions and ideas. Yet we sometimes keep the jewels of our minds to ourselves—and this is fine. Public recognition does not validate our intelligence and creativity; these exist regardless.

Let us treasure the high creations of our souls, and refuse to downgrade them because they will never be studied by others. Our creations are the gems in our private jewel box. We can admire them whenever we please.

On this day, I will take delight in my observations
and creative impulses.

August 8

RISK

So many people are afraid of taking even the smallest chance. They cling to dull routines as if those routines are life rafts.

Overheard at Junior's restaurant in Brooklyn

◄▐▌▐▌◄▐▌▐▌►

We go through our lives calculating risk. It may not even be a conscious accounting, because the tendency is automatic. We find comfort in what we know, and what we have; to risk it seems unwise and scary.

To be sure, weighing the risks involved in a situation is not a bad thing. Jumping into things just because they're new can become a reckless habit. But making progress necessarily entails risk.

On this day, I will remember a time I took a risk and something good came of it.

August 9

PREPARATION

*If you're going to play the game properly,
you'd better know every rule.*

—*Barbara Jordan*

If we haven't been in on the rule making—and generally we haven't—we may want to ignore the rule book altogether.

But life is rife with rules. There are rules at home, at work, in school—wherever we come into contact with others. Often rules are put in place to protect our rights. As we African-Americans have learned, they have also been enacted to abridge our rights.

Individually, we need to figure out which rules can and should be challenged. We may find that rules can be skirted or stretched when we accumulate power, but we're probably going to have to go along with most of them for a while if we're interested in acquiring that power.

*On this day, I will take five minutes to visualize that
I am negotiating the environment I need to master to
accomplish my goals.*

OBLIGATIONS

I am still learning—how to take joy in all the people I am, how to use all my selves in the service of what I believe, how to accept when I fail and rejoice when I succeed.

—AUDRE LORDE

It may take some doing to get into sync all our different "selves." The parent might be at odds with the artist, who might be in conflict with the lover, who fights for time with the athlete, breadwinner, and community activist.

Because we are many-faceted, evolving people, we have to cope with complex and conflicting needs and wants. It can be a juggling act: Different aspects will come to the fore while others recede. We can't expect to be all things to all people at all times. Perhaps the artist must take a backseat to the parent for a while. We can accept that and feel good about it because it is a choice we have made and value.

On this day, I will take five minutes to think about some of my most important obligations, and how I might more creatively go about using my time to fulfill them.

RECEPTIVITY

It is hard to talk about yourself all day. . . .
You learn when you're with other ideas, other
books, other friends. Talking about yourself
can't advance your life.

—YANNICK NOAH

Talking about ourselves—our lives, our feelings and experiences—can be fantastic. It can help us make sense of our actions, articulate our thoughts, work through our sadness, our emptiness, our confusion.

But we need to know when to pull out of ourselves, to say "Enough already!" How can we grow when we close ourselves to new information and input. When we have nothing new in our minds, it is no wonder we perceive our lives as boring and stale. Talk is fine; listening and looking, sublime!

On this day, I will read the front page of the
newspaper, read a magazine or a chapter from a
book, or have a conversation with somebody new and
really listen to him or her.

August 12

COURAGE

I am old enough to know that victory is often a thing deferred, and rarely at the summit of courage. . . . What is at the summit of courage, I think, is freedom. The freedom that comes with the knowledge that no earthly thing can break you.

—PAULA GIDDINGS

It may take years of struggle before we achieve the victory of which we daily dream. Some days can seem overwhelmingly grim. Those are the days when many of us drop out of the race.

But for those who are able to reach down deep and grab hold of some bit of courage, it is just another day. Challenging, yes. But in the act of rising above our disappointments, figuring out a new game plan, there is an emancipation of our spirit. We will not be stopped.

On this day, I will do at least one concrete thing that will advance me toward one of my goals.

August 13

GENERALIZING

I trust women. I was raised by women, by my godmother, my grandmother and my mother. . . . I understand women. I know women.

—ARSENIO HALL

We've heard people say these things: I know men. I know women. I know blacks. I know whites. We need to be careful. Mere proximity over an extended period of time only means we know—or think we know—*these* men, or *these* women.

Let's not smugly proclaim our understanding of any group of people but expect diversity and acknowledge the uniqueness inherent in each individual.

On this day, I will reflect upon one of the following: a woman I know; a man I know; a person of the same race or religion whom I know; a person of a different race or religion whom I know. Then I will take five minutes and note qualities that are unique to them or different from the stereotypical image of that kind of person.

ART

*Art is the material evidence that reminds us of
the wealth of our culture—of who we are.*
— MARY SCHMIDT CAMPBELL

If we view art as something foreign and unknowable,
it's no wonder we're intimidated.

We don't need to get pretentious when we talk
about or experience art. Art can move us, challenge
us, anger us. Art can be provocative or it can soothe
and sing to us.

When we welcome art into our lives, it can
enrich us in ways we hadn't anticipated. Art can inform us about our culture, instill pride, and encourage us to see the world differently. Art can show us
a bit of ourselves and help us define our experience.

Art isn't foreign; it is essential.

*On this day, I will take five minutes to look at and
appreciate a work of art created by an African or
African-American artist.*

August 15

CHOICES

Before me there were no actors in my family and no convicts.

—CHARLES DUTTON

Good or bad, we don't need to see it to become it. When we realize that our choices are our own and that no one is forcefully pointing us in one direction or another, we can choose our own path.

Knowing that he had spent more than seven years in prison, few would have guessed that Charles Dutton would go on to college, Yale Drama School, and then a rewarding career on stage and television. It's a good thing he heeded his own dreams and took advantage of the encouragement and opportunities that came his way.

Yes, influences are important, but we can pick and discard among those which are presented to us.

On this day, I will remember a time when I made a positive choice, and remember that positive choices will continue to present themselves to me throughout my life.

MISTAKES

There is a way to look at the past. Don't hide from it. It will not catch you if you don't repeat it.

—PEARL BAILEY

We are not always proud of ourselves. Sometimes we fail ourselves and others, too. It may be a specific action we lament, or general behavior that has caused the harm. Most of us can think of things in our lives that we wish we could now undo or that we would handle differently if we had a second chance. Maybe we hurt a romantic partner, were mean to our children, performed our jobs poorly, or succumbed to alcohol or drugs. Perhaps we allowed ourselves to drift without focus, and we'd give anything to have the time back to put it to better use.

We make mistakes. The best way to handle them is not to take guilt as our constant companion, not to spend our lives grieving, but to vow to live differently from here on out.

On this day, I will take five minutes to focus on the present, and to realize that my past is neither my present nor my future.

VALUES

Work must be inspired by the right ideals, and education must not simply teach work, but life based on those ideals.

—W.E.B. DU BOIS

In this book we talk about the importance of hard work. We also want to underscore the importance of having an underlying sense of the values for which we're working. Without a higher purpose to our work, our salary and the goodies we can spend it on become our sole purpose.

Sometimes we lose track of what we're working on and what we're working for, so from time to time it behooves us to stop and see how and what we're doing.

We must also remember our community. With our ideals in mind, if we have the cash to buy a luxury car, we should certainly have a small amount to donate to a black charity.

On this day, I will work with pencil and notebook in an effort to compare facets of the way I am living my life with my underlying values.

August 18

FRIENDSHIP

An enemy slaughters, a friend distributes.
—*FULFULDE proverb*

◼▦◻▦◼

Who are our friends? Do they support and applaud our endeavors, or begrudge our ambition and success? Do they want to listen, or only to talk? Do they consider our needs and feelings, or only their own? Do they stay beside us in our grief, our despair, our disappointment, or go on to someone who is more cheerful or successful?

We need to select our friends with care—and treasure those friendships based on sincerity and mutual support.

On this day, I will do something for an African-American colleague, friend, acquaintance, or family member. I might buy him/her a cup of coffee, compliment him/her on the day's choice of apparel, or simply express happiness that he/she is around and part of my life.

August 19

HASTE

Before shooting, one must aim.

—*NIGERIAN proverb*

Fulfilling goals isn't easy, but it's even harder if you don't know what your goals are. Make sure you know what you want before you rush out to get it.

On this day, I will do at least one thing that brings me closer to attaining one of my goals.

August 20

BALANCE

I was the best . . . and it was a drag. Now I just want to be good, and stay good.

—EDDIE MURPHY

Aiming to be "the best" sounds like a worthy goal. But being the best requires great sacrifice, necessitating that we subjugate other aspects of ourselves in order to focus on our high-reaching goal. Becoming the best doctor, salesman, writer, or comedian can mean years of relegating personal relationships and other areas of interest and concern to secondary status. Can we wait till we've reached our "best" to fulfill our other wants and needs?

Maybe we need to rethink what it means to be the best. Doing *our* best may not win the kind of recognition and superstardom that being *the* best confers, but it means we have recognized our complexity and sought to balance all our goals.

On this day, I will take five minutes to note and appreciate the good things about myself.

August 21

MENTAL AND PHYSICAL HEALTH

The head and the body must serve each other.
—From a WOLOF folktale

When the body is healthy, the mind is free to roam in positive directions, to be creative and find stimulation. But if the body is wracked with pain, burdened by stress or obesity or in some other dysfunctional state, the mind will be distracted by its aches and discomforts.

Likewise, when the mind is fraught with anxiety, negativity, or depression, we are probably not focused on doing all the proper things to keep the body healthy. We may eat or drink too much, smoke, fail to exercise, and neglect nutrition and stress management.

Let us not underestimate the way the parts influence the whole. We need to be aware of any glitches throughout our mind-body system that can undermine our whole performance.

On this day, I will take five minutes to review my dietary habits to determine if I am eating a healthy, balanced diet. If not, I pledge to modify my meals so that they are conducive to a healthy body and mind.

August 22

STRUGGLE

*People don't understand the kind of fight it
takes to record what you want to record the
way you want to record it.*

—BILLIE HOLIDAY

Living to realize your dreams takes fighting, and lots
of it. An aspiring singer, for example, may have to
fight her parents who want her to get a business degree, her music teachers who say she is not ready,
her boyfriend, her other obligations, and her own
self-doubts. And that's just in *starting* her career!

After a time we might wonder if we're up for
it, if we still have the energy and stamina. Perhaps
it would be easier to back down.

If our goals mean anything to us, we will not
give up easily. We *do* need to be prepared, mentally
and physically. But knowing how others fought and
won can inspire us to keep pressing forward.

*On this day, I will relax and recall a time I felt like
giving up but continued at my task.*

August 23

PROGRESS

*We ask not that others bear our burden, but do
not obstruct our pathway, and we will throw off
our burdens as we run.*

—REVERDY RANSOM

Yet people have stood in our way and, incredulously,
bellowed, "Why aren't you moving? Why aren't you
making progress?"

We need to learn about the progress our people
have made so that we do not grow disheartened by
constant suggestions that we are inept and unmoti-
vated. Today we still have our burdens—poverty, in-
ferior education, drugs, crime, and bigotry. Some of
us feel overwhelmed by our frustrations. These are
not hardships we can cast off overnight.

But burdens can be lightened, bit by bit. And
our strength can grow, bit by bit. It takes commitment and passion. Energy begets energy. We are not
powerless; we have merely to tap into the power
within us and learn how to use it efficiently.

*On this day, I will take five minutes to tap into my
inner power and visualize myself accomplishing one of
my goals.*

August 24

VISUALIZATION

Some people are your relatives but others are your ancestors, and you choose the ones you want to have as ancestors. You create yourself out of those values.

—RALPH ELLISON

Our pool of ancestors is vast. When we take time to study our history, we need to recognize the individual greatness, dignity, and style of our ancestors—and use their lives as models for our own.

On this day, I will read a book of black history or a chapter in the autobiography of a great black man or a woman.

August 25

THINKING SMART

The issue is no longer where you sit on the bus or whether you can drive it; it's whether you can develop the capital to own the bus company.

—WILLIAM H. GRAY III

We see that to change things, we need more control, more power and influence. So when we think about where our education will take us, our ultimate goal ought to be how we can best utilize our talents while seeking to make the most of life's opportunities.

We've seen that our communities do not develop through anyone's effort but our own. That means we're going to have to provide more goods and services to ourselves, to build on what we have already, and to patronize our own businesses and institutions. At the same time, we must infiltrate the so-called mainstream to have input and impact on every aspect of American life.

On this day, I will do something to help or give encouragement to a fellow African-American.

August 26

LOOKING BACK

Don't look back. Something might be gaining on you.

—LEROY "SATCHEL" PAIGE

><

Lingering on events out of our past prevents us from living here and now. When we keep looking back, we cannot look ahead, which puts us in danger of missing opportunities or losing hope for better things to come.

When we look back to our old failures—attempts at losing weight, finding romance, landing jobs, or finishing projects we started—we risk succumbing to the belief that our failures define us. But who we are is who we now choose to be—successful, competent, wise, and wonderful.

When we make mistakes or do not achieve the success we'd anticipated, let's examine our actions *at that moment,* then take our lessons with us and move on. The future will become the present, so we need to anticipate and prepare for it.

On this day, I will do at least one thing that will help me accomplish one of my goals.

August 27

CYCLES

By going and coming, a bird weaves its nest.
—ASHANTI *proverb, West Africa*

We watch the bird fly away and may be fooled into thinking that it has abandoned its work. But a nest is not built if the materials are not sought and brought back to the tree.

There are times when we must get away from our work in order to locate the resources we need to complete it. We may require new information or inspiration, or simply a break in which to rest and refresh our spirit. We don't need to feel guilty for these times and we should resist the taunts of others who do not understand our work habits or needs.

As long as we get back to our task, as long as we do not lose sight of our ultimate goal, we can fly away with impunity.

On this day, I will take five minutes to remember that there is a cycle to life, and the fact that I am not always on the scene does not mean that I am not on the job.

SELF-RESPECT

*One cannot give to a person that which he
already possesses.*

—TOUSSAINT L'OUVERTURE,
Proclamation, March 1, 1802

Dignity, self-respect—no one can bestow these upon
us. Pride in ourselves can come only from within.
Looking outside ourselves for validation means we're
looking in the wrong place and opens us up to being
frustrated or misled.

It may feel wonderful when, through our accomplishments, we gain the respect of our friends,
our families, or our co-workers. But what they're ad-
miring is the result of qualities that have been there
all along, way before the promotion, the new hair-
style, the plum job offer, the new house.

There are some who may never regard us well,
but as long as we love and respect ourselves, their
opinions cannot hold us back.

*On this day, for no more than five minutes, I will
repeat silently to myself: "I am a lovable and worthy
person. I am generous, intelligent, and creative."*

August 29

POSITIVE THOUGHTS

If I walked a perfect line, there'd be people who said I was too perfect. . . . There will always be naysayers, but I won't give them free rent in my head.

—CARL LEWIS

There are occasionally people in our lives who cannot be pleased. Whatever we do is wrong. Whatever we say is arguable or offensive. When we get on this difficult and contrary track with someone close to us, we've got a problem.

It takes a strong mind to keep out all the negative voices. We are, throughout our lives, doubted, criticized, and challenged. We must steel ourselves against the voices that would pull us down or mislead us. When we fill our minds with positive thoughts, we leave no room for the ones that can hurt us.

At the end of this day, I will take five minutes to remember at least one good thing that happened to me, or something I did that gave me pleasure or satisfaction.

August 30

REVENGE

It is Martin King who taught that a real moral struggle seeks to win partners, not to leave victims.

— MAULANA KARENGA

When we consider what has happened and continues to happen to us in this country, it's not easy to quell the rage inside. Every time we take a step forward, it seems there is a systemic push to force us two steps back. As we gain power, there are times we might be tempted to take revenge.

Yet, if we are bent on retribution, we are not using our energy efficiently. We need to be forging alliances and building something for ourselves. This holds true on a personal level as well. If someone hurts us, we can't allow them to become the focus of all our thoughts.

Occasionally, we've got to take an emotional step or two back in order to keep what is most important in focus.

On this day, and only for today, I pledge to put all feuds behind me and focus on doing at least one thing that will advance me toward my goal.

WORRY

Many people worry, but they don't do anything about it.

—PEARL BAILEY

Yes, many of us are constant worriers. We worry about making the rent next month and about paying off the credit card. We worry about our health, our sanity, our jobs, our safety.

What does all this worrying accomplish? Perhaps a few more gray hairs, slightly deeper frown lines, a weight gain or loss, sleep deprivation, and a state of inner agitation that can give us an ulcer or worse.

Addressing our worries with positive action is our only recourse. If we need more money, how can we make it? If we fear for our children's safety, how can we move to a better neighborhood? It may take some time to overcome our difficulties, but each step taken in that direction will help slow the worry machine inside us.

On this day, I will take five minutes to focus on an issue that is troubling me—and then I will devise baby steps toward fixing it.

September 1

PRIDE

*Don't be ashamed to show your colors,
and to own them.*

—WILLIAM WELLS BROWN

It is wonderful to be different. Good thing, since we *all* are. We are noisy, quiet, scientific, buoyant, thoughtful, extroverted, introverted, dreamy, decisive people.

Not only must we not be ashamed of our particular attributes, we must work *with* them, using them to propel us through life. A soft-spoken, meticulous person is as necessary to the mix as a brash, boisterous person. Both these people, for instance, can make highly effective and successful lawyers, or artists, or bakers, or salespeople.

Let us rejoice in our colors, and allow others to rejoice in theirs.

On this day, I will take five minutes to visualize myself as successful in two different situations using my unique attributes and talents.

September 2

SUCCESS

You can't hurry up good times by waitin' for 'em.
—*U.S. proverb*

Sometimes we get the idea we can coast along until we eventually bump into our good times. It might be that we are waiting for others to spot our talent and shower rewards upon us. We don't always realize or like to hear that we've got to do more than our work to get ahead. We may have to look for mentors, make our ambitions known, or socialize with folks we don't love.

Simply waiting for our rewards can have us waiting forever.

On this day, I will make a list of all the necessary steps it will take for me to accomplish one of my goals.

September 3

PARENTS

I cannot forget my mother. Though not as sturdy as others, she is my bridge. When I needed to get across, she steadied herself long enough for me to run across safely.

—RENITA WEEMS

Some of us are blessed from the start. We have loving, concerned parents who try to do their best for us. Some of us are challenged from the start. Parents die. Parents leave. Parents stay, unable for whatever reason to fulfill their roles and give us what we desperately need. Parents we want to trust hurt us.

It is important to acknowledge that we are not our parents. We can be inspired by the best in them, but we are not condemned to repeat their mistakes or live their lives. Ultimately, we must be equipped to nurture ourselves with love and understanding.

On this day, I will take five minutes to meditate on my parents or on the adults who have been parent figures to me. I will note how we are different, and how we are similar.

September 4

VISIBILITY

You've got to find a way to make people know you're there.

—NIKKI GIOVANNI

Life demands our presence. Letting people know we're here is crucial, whether in terms of making career gains, in letting our families know we care, or in sending a message to our elected officials.

We can advertise our presence by joining professional organizations or by networking to meet others—of all ethnicities—with whom we can exchange valuable career information. If we have children, we can get involved with school and PTA functions, as our time allows. This lets both teachers and administration know of our active interest in our child's education. Even sending a holiday card to our child's teacher can have a subtle impact.

In invisibility, there is little, if any, power. Our active presence has influence. Let's use it.

On this day, I will make my presence known by either starting up a light conversation, presenting an idea, spending time with a family member or in some other way.

September 5

FLEXIBILITY AND ACHIEVEMENT

Necessity has no law.
—TERENCE, from The Eunuch, *Act V*

There are lots of unwritten rules we are expected to follow. Add to that all our personal "can'ts" and "shouldn'ts" and it's no wonder a lot of us are frustrated.

We need to learn to break free from the restrictions that bind us—the internal stop signs and the narrow expectations of others. Accomplishment in any form requires that we know when to buck convention and find more creative solutions. This improvisational style calls for a certain daring, which African-Americans have exhibited in countless ways over the years. We have flouted convention and put our personal stamp on science, athletics, music, and literature. To put our own style into all the things we do, we just need to dare!

On this day, I will take five minutes and listen to a piece of music, study a scientific achievement, read a paragraph of literature, or look at a piece of art— whatever happens to be available in my house—and meditate on the relationship of individual style and achievement.

PERSEVERANCE

Ev'ry day fishin' day, but no ev'ry day catch fish.
—BAHAMIAN proverb

Every day we walk to our spots, bait our hooks, cast our lines. Some days there's not even a nibble to give us hope. It can be frustrating, but we've got to get up and do it all over again the next day or else there definitely won't be any fish for dinner.

Perhaps we need to make sure of our timing. Come too early or too late, the fish won't be there. Let's check our bait, too, to see if it's fat enough. Still, maybe it's time to reel in and go find another spot.

The point is, we don't give up. We've got to go on fishing for our dreams. There may be long stretches where we go home with empty pails. That's okay, as long as we don't lose faith. There's the catch of a lifetime out there waiting for us if we are persistent and smart.

On this day, I will take five minutes to focus on one
of my goals and imagine myself making any
adjustments that might be necessary to make it a
reality.

SELF-PITY

But before my thoughts led me further in the direction of self-pity, I brought them to a halt, reminding myself that this was precisely what solitary confinement was supposed to evoke.

—ANGELA DAVIS

Self-pity is a trap most of us know all too well. It often occurs when we are stagnating and feel we cannot change our condition, that the forces against us are too strong to fight. When we do not see a way out of a bad situation, or have not seriously looked for one, it is no wonder we feel so sorry for ourselves.

Yet there is nothing productive to come out of self-pity. If anything, it wastes time that could be put to better use, focusing on ways to solve the problem. Self-pity drags us down, reiterating our worst fears about ourselves—that we are inept or undeserving of better.

Figuring out our next step can put an end to self-pity. We always have options; we just need to be able to see them.

On this day, I will focus on something I feel is impeding me. Then I will spend five minutes figuring out a way around the impediment.

HUMOR

*If you don't have a sense of humor, you become
a scowling time bomb, striking out at people
who are dear to you.*

—ISHMAEL REED

One of the most pleasant means of stress relief is
humor. It's free, conveniently located, and has no
harmful side effects. We don't have to tell jokes or
do impersonations—we just need to find the humor
and absurdity always present in life.

We have a lot to deal with. Sometimes things
look pretty grave. There are times when we've got to
show we're serious. But it helps to let down our
guard—and laugh.

*On this day, I will find humor in something that I let
get to me, such as not being able to get a jar open or
misplacing my keys.*

September 9

MOMENTUM

The sight of freedom looming on the horizon
should encourage us to redouble our efforts.
— NELSON MANDELA

Finding ourselves close to our goals, we are some-times tempted to coast. We lose momentum, and our goals can begin to slip away from us. After a while, we may lose hope—it's taking too long, too much energy, too much commitment. We may begin to question the value of our goals or our worthiness to achieve them.

Let's resist the temptation to ease up in the pursuit of our goals. When we feel them looming on our horizon, we need to keep moving steadily forward to capture them. Redoubling our efforts will ensure that no time or energy is wasted.

On this day, I will make some small but concrete
gesture toward accomplishing one of my goals.

September 10

BLACK PRIDE

*Racism should make us [African-Americans]
love one another, not disrespect or murder each
other.*

—JAMES GOODWIN

This former gang-leader-turned-repertory-theater-
director points out that "we have to take some of the
responsibility and blame" for our problems. Sure,
racism exists, but we hurt ourselves if we use it to
absolve ourselves for our own destructive actions.
Who ultimately picks up the gun or the needle?

On a personal level, racism cannot be an excuse for us not to pursue our dreams and make
wholesome choices for our lives. When there are
those who would lock us up, send us off, or reduce
us with every opportunity, we have more reason to
strengthen our community, to love and support each
other.

*On this day, I will take five minutes to look at
something speaking to my pride in my heritage—my
"X" cap, my family photos, African cloth—and let
its lingering mental image inspire me to excellence.*

September 11

EXCELLENCE

*Show me someone content with mediocrity and
I'll show you someone destined for failure.*
— JOHNETTA COLE

It is never too late to trade in mediocrity for excellence. Diligence and a positive mental outlook are tools we can acquire, hone, and put to use if we decide to choose a life that will stimulate and gratify us.

*On this day, I will spend five minutes remembering
something I did in the past that made me proud.
Then I will visualize how I could have made it better.*

September 12

MOODINESS

Yes, I can be moody. I can be bitchy. . . . But when I'm moody and bitchy, I keep my butt at home.

—ANITA BAKER

We all have our lousy moods—days when all we want to do is kick everything in our path. We prove we can yell, grunt, sneer, insult, explode, and needle with the best of them. Yet life and duty and social obligations beckon. There are the innocent expectations of unsuspecting children, spouses, lovers, friends, parents, and co-workers.

Please, let us spare these innocent people! We have no right to vent our moods on them. There are options: Stay home or stay clear, punch a pillow, go for a walk. Discover what works for *you*. You'll have nothing to apologize for later.

On this day, I will take five minutes to visualize myself dealing with a bad mood in a socially responsible way.

SEX

*Heaven and earth! How is it
that bodies join but never
meet?*

—BEAH RICHARDS

We have heard before how empty sex can be when the parties involved have few, if any, feelings for each other, and how exquisite it is within a loving relationship.

But even in loving relationships, we can feel as if we're just going through the motions. When sex disappoints, as it can when we are fatigued, depressed, or preoccupied, we wonder what is wrong in our relationship.

We must understand that sex can enhance love, but is not love itself. A great physical attraction does not ensure spiritual chemistry; but a connection of souls adds passion and meaning to our love-making.

On this day, I pledge to take five minutes to carefully determine my needs in my relationship, and to voice those needs to my partner.

September 14

DIRECTION

The way she wastes her time, the way she drifts through the office, you feel that all she wants to do with her life is to lose it somewhere.

—Black executive
about one of his employees

It is not uncommon on occasion to find ourselves drifting. Perhaps we stay too long in an unpromising relationship or an unrewarding job. It happens.

When drifting becomes a life-style, however, our lives lose purpose. When we abandon the helm and cut the engine, there is little left to do but view the scenery as it passes.

We need to make sure that we are in charge of our lives, that we have direction. Through constant evaluation, we can check our course and determine whether we need to make adjustments.

On this day, I will take five minutes to think about the direction and purpose of my life, and decide if I am being efficient in getting there.

September 15

PROGRESS

We must not, in trying to think about how we can make a big difference, ignore the small daily differences we can make which, over time, add up to big differences that we often cannot foresee.

—MARIAN WRIGHT EDELMAN

The encouraging words and gestures we daily make to our loved ones and to others in our community are as significant and meaningful as any achievement that wins public kudos and history-book recognition. Let us not discount our very real personal power and the effect we can have on others' lives. The love we convey to our children and our fervent and articulated belief in them can be magical and awesome. Volunteering our time to those in need, voting, joining the PTA, learning more about our communities and working to address their problems may not win us awards that make the six o'clock news, but they hold countless rewards if we open our eyes to them.

On this day, I will congratulate a loved one—a sibling, a lover, a child, for instance—upon the completion of some routine activity—such as doing homework—that advances them toward one of their goals.

INSPIRATION

*As I grow older, part of my emotional survival
plan must be to actively seek inspiration instead
of passively waiting for it to find me.*
—BEBE MOORE CAMPBELL

We can spend our whole lives waiting for good things
to come to us. After a while, though, we're apt to
think we're just not lucky. Perhaps we begin to doubt
ourselves when we note our peers claiming their rewards while we are still wondering what happened to
ours.

We can avoid the twin problems of stagnation
and disappointment if we are not only open to but
actively solicitous of information and inspiration. A
curious and hungry mind ensures that there is constant input, enabling us to think, analyze, and learn.
But the secret is a commitment to action, to putting
newfound knowledge—whether from book, talk
show, or sermon—to use.

Let's learn to look for what we need; there is
a lot to inspire us if we are determined to find it.

*On this day, I will do at least one concrete thing that
advances me toward one of my goals.*

September 17

SELF-DETERMINATION

*I don't see why we can't be good in one thing
and try to experiment in being good at another.*
— NAOMI CAMPBELL

People have a habit of looking at us and seeing what
we are now, not what we could be. Perhaps it's because most people—parents, spouses, friends in-
cluded—want to be able to pin things down a certain
way in order to feel comfortable. Challenging their
perceptions of us throws them off balance.

When we allow other people's opinions to re-
strict us, we are limiting our options and our chances
at self-fulfillment.

Only we know who we are. There is growth in
experimentation. Let's refuse to stagnate in order to
please others.

*On this day, I will take five minutes to be quiet and
listen to my inner self, and determine who I am and
what I should be.*

September 18

APPROPRIATENESS

When the music changes, so does the dance.

—HAUSA proverb

We need to acknowledge that there is dinner-table conversation and bedroom conversation, times to turn up the music and times for silence, times to argue and times to hold our comments, a place for quiet work and a place for partying.

On this day, I will tune in to the environment around me and the emotions within me and act appropriately.

September 19

CHANGE

Life is like an enormous darkened room in which somebody keeps moving the furniture; you can't tell from moment to moment whether you're about to plop into your favorite easy chair or a potted cactus.

—ERIC V. COPAGE

The reality is, things shift and change all the time in our lives. "Facts" change. Alliances shift. Rules are rewritten. Values are cast off and replaced by new ones. Expertise is challenged or termed fraudulent. Fashions come and go.

We may not always find the soft cushion; we are not infallible. But we must learn to trust our intuition, our instinct for what is right.

I trust my intuition to help guide me through the changing circumstances of this world. On this day, I will take five minutes to remember a time when my intuition led me to something good.

CENSORING OURSELVES

*A lot of times we censor ourselves before the
censor even gets there.*

—SPIKE LEE

We need to stop thinking up reasons why our dreams
cannot work, and focus on what we can do to *make*
them work. If there are obstacles, how can we get
around them? If we need help or expertise, where
can we get it?

We are capable of so much if we resist our
internal censors and tap into the inventiveness and
conviction that can make our dreams reality.

*On this day, I will contemplate the biggest obstacles
preventing me from attaining one of my goals. Then I
will take five minutes to think of different ways of
getting over, around, under, or through that obstacle.
I will not self-censor; I will entertain even what seems
at first blush totally inane ideas.*

EXCELLENCE

Who I am is the best I can be.
—LEONTYNE PRICE

▰▰▰▰▰

When we can make this claim, our lives are well lived. Being "the best we can be" does not imply we have reached all our goals but only that we are working as hard as we can *toward* those goals. It means using our talents well.

Paradoxically, being "the best I can be" also leaves room for improvement. No person alive is perfect. We have our faults and weaknesses. We also have limits on our time and energy. We have obligations, responsibilities, and priorities. We can forgive ourselves for not learning French or how to cook as long as we are loving parents and hardworking and generous individuals.

We need to assess our lives and consider what *we* need to accomplish in order to live life fully in a way that satisfies *us*.

On this day, I will take five minutes to write out a strategy that will enable me to accomplish one of my goals.

SELF-WORTH

*The price of your hat isn't the measure of
your brain.*

—*AFRICAN-AMERICAN proverb*

African-Americans have long realized that worth has
nothing to do with station in life. We have grandparents who were not able to become doctors, lawyers, engineers, and scientists—not because of any
lack of ability but because racism held them back.

Yet too often now we dishonor our grandparents by judging each other on the basis of superfi-
cialities such as our job, degree of fame, sphere of
influence, or paycheck size. Let's judge others by the
content of their souls—not by any other criteria.

*On this day, I will choose one likely African-
American, and begin the long process of forging an
alliance based on trust. Or I will take an African-
American I am beginning to trust and suggest we get
together over coffee.*

September 23

POWER

You can either try to get inside and have some influence, or you can stay outside and be pure and powerless.

—JAMES BROWN

Yes, it's important to maintain our sense of integrity; it's also important to get the job done. It depends on our agenda. Can we stay "outside" and still have the power we need to do what we must? Staying outside just to complain how crooked it is inside won't help.

Once we have some power and influence, we can change things. African-Americans need more control; let's consider all the ways (from outside and in) we have to acquire power.

On this day, I will do at least one thing that will advance me toward one of my goals, and I know that I will be able to do this and maintain my integrity.

September 24

SELFISHNESS

Sometimes you give so much that it hurts. You give and give and give, and you have nothing that belongs to you. It's important to have something that belongs to you . . . something inside you, to keep to yourself.

—YANNICK NOAH

▰▰▰▰▰▰

We are brought up to be generous and considerate. We give to our jobs, to our romantic partners, to our friends, parents, and children. We give to strangers who may be less fortunate, and to social and political causes. What do we have left after all our giving? Have we remembered to keep something for ourselves?

We all need to give a little to ourselves and denying ourselves those things that make us feel good can drain us in the long run. Let's not feel guilty about keeping a part of ourselves *for* ourselves.

On this day, I will take five minutes to think about what I want to do with my life. Do I feel productive? Fulfilled? What can I do that will increase my sense of satisfaction and accomplishment?

September 25

FLEXIBILITY/PURPOSE

By any means necessary.

—MALCOLM X

"By any means necessary" means just that. It means being, by turns, inventive, rude, obstinate, bold, reclusive, wily—if the situation calls for it. "By any means necessary" means you don't always have to try to be polite. We should pursue our endeavors—whether for true freedom and political empowerment, a promotion at work, or better schooling for our children—with a mixture of passion, perseverance and intelligence, which are summed up by the phrase "By any means necessary."

On this day, I will think about the most difficult part of accomplishing one of my goals. And then I will take five minutes to think of a solution to it, and I will seriously consider each solution no matter how strange or impractical it seems.

September 26

HERITAGE

The fruit must have a stem before it grows.
—JABO proverb, Liberia

We all have stems. We all have roots—our parents, our grandparents, our ancestors. While it may be exceedingly difficult to trace our family tree back very far, obscured as it may be by the torturous divisions of families in slavery—let alone pinpoint our beginnings in Africa—we can learn of the greatness of our people.

If we study our complete history, we see that we have been an industrious and ingenious people in very trying circumstances. We learn, by example, the importance of fighting, of perseverance, and of not losing hope.

Let us also look to those who have raised us, and note the good that we can emulate. What we learn about ourselves, we must then pass on in order to help our own fruit grow.

On this day, I will take five minutes to think about someone who helped me, who has taken an interest in me. And I will thank him or her.

MODESTY

Let's not get too full of ourselves. Let's leave space for God to come into the room.

—QUINCY JONES

While we strive to love and value ourselves, we may occasionally lapse into arrogance or become overly judgmental or derisive of others. A little self-centeredness can be a blessing and an aid; too much and we don't allow ourselves room to grow or improve.

Let's learn to love ourselves, but save our worshiping for church. Loving ourselves does not require that we devalue others. When we do that, our abilities to empathize, to share, to generate kindness and concern wither. It's okay to dream of superstardom, but that cannot be our whole identity or we become caricatures instead of whole persons.

On this day, I will choose something that I do very well and strive to do it better.

September 28

KINDNESS

*My father, as an adult, did not go to church,
but he was kinder than swarms of church-goers.*
—*GWENDOLYN BROOKS*

The measure of our kindness is taken from our every-day acts—the way we treat our children, mate, co-workers, and strangers on the street. Some of us think kindness indicates a weakness—only suckers are kind, and they get taken advantage of for their naiveté.

Why be kind? Simply because it feels good. It affirms life and our humanity. On a practical level, our kindness may be returned by those around us now or later in our lives. And, lastly, we simply know that we *should* be kind. It is the decent, moral way to live.

*On this day, I pledge to be kind in whatever
manageable ways I can to those I care for.*

September 29

UNITY

*There is no separate freedom or dignity for
African men and women.*

—MAULANA KARENGA

Of course, neither black men nor black women can
be truly free unless both are free.

And as comfortable and removed as any African-American may be, we all know that a bigot will
not bother to ask our job title and financial status
before firing his gun or kicking us in the head. It
can happen to us; it can happen to our children.

When a racist crime occurs, we must join with
our community to demand justice.

We need to accumulate both individual and
collective economic power, which will enable us to
fund candidates who will work for us.

*On this day, I pledge to encourage and support other
African-Americans in their endeavors.*

September 30

VISION

*I had to practically hypnotize myself into
thinking I was going to be a success.*
—JOHN SINGLETON

To be successful in whatever we do, we must first
have a vision of ourselves as successful. From day to
day, we must keep that vision alive, even when we
occasionally feel we've acted in ways antithetical to
our vision.

It's easy to see how this works in terms of career success. But perhaps our vision is one of ourselves as a successful parent. Picturing ourselves as
patient, tolerant individuals engaging in a stimulating and engaging interaction with our child can give
us something to work toward. And even while we may
still lose our temper or become impatient with our
child, we recover faster and have fewer lapses when
we keep our ideal in mind.

Let's hypnotize ourselves into the healthy,
happy, productive people we want to be.

*On this day, I will consider my vision of myself or
my life and do at least one concrete thing that
advances me toward that vision.*

October 1

BLACKNESS

*Don't say I don't have soul or what you
consider to be "Blackness." I know what my
color is.*

—WHITNEY HOUSTON

What *is* our idea of being black anyway? What's our
definition of soul? James Brown, most will agree, has
soul to spare. Does James DePriest, music director
of the Oregon Symphony?

When does a person qualify as black? If someone is "not black enough" for our tastes, does that
mean someone else can be "too black"?

This business gets absurd. Our backgrounds,
looks, life-styles, and experiences are incredibly varied. It only hurts us to limit ourselves.

Let's look to our common roots and forget
about branding our people according to our perceptions of their blackness.

*On this day, I will take five minutes to reflect upon
the varied nature of black people, our many styles and
contributions.*

October 2

DISCRETION

The discreet man knows how to hold his tongue.
—MALAGASY proverb

For so many years, African-Americans were denied the right to take a stand and be heard. Now, it seems, we're making up for it with a vengeance. "Tell it like it is" was, after all, one of *our* slogans. Determined never again to swallow the indignity of having our voices stifled, we pride ourselves on our honesty—sometimes to a fault.

Is it so necessary to burst another's bubble with our opinion? Nothing wrong with dissension, of course. Debate is a healthy exercise. But on some issues, it may be kinder to hold back a bit. If, for instance, a friend is delighted with a new job, dress, or boyfriend, what does it accomplish for us to blast it, or him?

We need to look inside to determine our own motivations in such instances. Perhaps we're jealous. Understanding that can spare a friendship.

While honesty can be beautiful, it can also be brutal.
On this day, I will try to be sensitive to times when
discretion is the nobler way to go.

CHALLENGES

*Go all the way to the edge, don't settle
for a safe position.*

—CORDELL REAGON

We often opt for the safer course in life even when
the harder or riskier one sounds more exciting and
rewarding to us. These are times when we need to
determine whether it's wisdom or fear that is moti-
vating us in our choices. If it's fear, we don't need
to succumb. We can practice taking small risks first;
we'll get gutsier as we get used to the feeling out at
the edge. After a while, safety will feel downright
oppressive!

*I am strong. I am smart. I am resilient. On this
day, I will take five minutes to remember a time when
I was in a challenging situation and triumphed.*

October 4

SELF-DETERMINATION

*Stand on your own two Black feet and fight
like hell for your place in the world. . . .*

—AMY JACQUES GARVEY

What is our place in the world? Our parents might have one notion, our spouse another, and white people a third—and none might have a thing to do with our own idea of "our place."

Often we find ourselves fighting those who believe they know what's best for us, and yet they may be driven by their own concerns.

Defining ourselves takes work. Living true to ourselves requires fight and stamina. On our own two Black feet, we might bend and sway and even hunker over once in a while, but as long as we're still standing, we can have hope, because, in this position, we can go forward and make progress.

*On this day, I will take five minutes to visualize
myself succeeding at one of my goals.*

NUTRITION

The empty bag cannot stand up.
—HAITIAN proverb

So said the hungry enslaved African when scolded for idleness. Let's extend this proverb to apply not merely to food but to a nutritious diet that will enable us to live productive and satisfying lives.

We simply cannot live up to life's challenges when we are malnourished. We must learn to feed ourselves right and, by all means, feed our children right. Sound nutritional advice can be found in library books, in newspapers, and in current magazines. Let's avoid faddish diets and use common sense: We need vegetables, fruits, and grains every day.

Let's not use lack of money and time as excuses for poor eating habits; a bowl of oatmeal and orange juice at home costs less than the daily doughnut and coffee. It is *we* who deal ourselves disadvantages when we eat nutritionally bankrupt foods.

On this day, I will take five minutes to review my dietary habits, and if I find them lacking, I pledge to modify my meals so that they are conducive to a healthy body and mind.

October 6

WHITE PEOPLE

*I believe there are some sincere white people.
But I think they should prove it.*

—MALCOLM X

Some of us spend a lot of time thinking about white people and trying to figure out our personal attitude toward them. Should we trust them, and how far? Can we really be friends? Others of us have a ready answer to that question—no!

Do we really need to take a position on this? The sincerity, or lack of it, of any individual will out eventually. To assume a person's decency from the start can needlessly endanger us; to reject it can handicap us, perhaps preventing us from establishing a mutually beneficial and rewarding relationship.

*I trust my judgment of people and will take
relationships one step at a time. I will allow my
intuition about people to work, knowing that the good
or ill of those around me will be revealed.*

October 7

DEPRESSION

*Most people who are depressed have a legitimate
reason to be. There's a healthy part of your ego
that tells you something's not right. The
problem with depression is that it can become
generalized to encompass your entire existence.*

—CRAIG K. POLITE

Depression can make it hard to get out of bed in the
morning, hard to share joy with friends and family,
hard to care about ourselves the way we ought to.
Dr. Polite recommends pinpointing exactly what is
wrong in our lives and finding ways to manage that
problem so it doesn't overwhelm our general outlook
and well-being.

*On this day, I will also do something to help me
advance toward one of my goals.*

October 8

APPRECIATION

The one being carried does not realize how far away the town is.

—*NIGERIAN proverb*

Until we are adults—perhaps with children of our own—we usually do not realize the extent to which our parents sacrificed for us, how hard they worked, and the number of hours they devoted to our development. Until we study the history and struggles of our people, we do not begin to fathom the amount of effort our ancestors exerted and the cruelty they endured and over which they triumphed.

Knowledge of the effort required to carry us this distance should propel us in the right direction and help us bear up under our own burdens. Continuing the struggle is the best way we have of saying thank you to those who struggled for us.

On this day, I will remember those who came before me and who sacrificed to make available the opportunities I have. I pledge to use my creativity and faith to avail myself of those opportunities and do the best I can at today's tasks.

October 9

SELF-LOVE

*I have always lived well, bought fresh flowers
and eaten filet mignon.*

—TERRY MCMILLAN

Who says we can't treat ourselves? We spend so
much of our time being the conscientious employee,
the supportive spouse or mate, the nurturing parent
or the dutiful son or daughter that we sometimes let
our own needs slide. We get the idea in our heads
that flowers and luxury food are for special occasions.
Aren't *we* special? Besides, it's the normal humdrum
days when we need to brighten things up a bit.

Doing something nice for ourselves gives us a
sense of control over our lives. Yes, we *can* make a
difference. And we are *worth* fussing over. Without
bankrupting ourselves or pushing our credit lines to
the limit, we can give ourselves regular valentines
that remind us that life is enjoyable.

*On this day, I will treat myself to something special
that I love. I deserve it.*

October 10

ORIGINALITY

When I was doing my talk show in Baltimore,
I used to watch Donahue to figure out how to
do it. That's the truth. I stopped . . . because I
found myself saying, "Is the caller there?"—
and repeating things just the way he did.

—OPRAH WINFREY

On the way to developing our own style, it can be very useful to study those we admire in our field. Learning all we can about a role model's career path can give us insight into what we may need to do to accomplish our goals.

What we're looking for are techniques that we can adapt to suit our own strengths and abilities. No one should strive to become a carbon copy of someone else, because we can lose the best part of ourselves that way. But let's acknowledge that we can learn and benefit by the example of others. Over time our own style evolves.

On this day, I will take five minutes to remember how
I learned by imitating the way someone I admired did
something. Then I will reflect upon the way I do it
now and the personal stamp I have brought to it.

TRADITION

The young cannot teach tradition to the old.
—YORUBA proverb

Our children are our hope, and our future. We need to provide them with the tools they will require to live productive and healthy lives. But how can we do this unless *we* are willing to live this way? "Do as I say and not as I do" simply does not work.

We needn't be parents to desire a better world for our people. Our achievements and our involvement can inspire many, and we may never realize it.

Tradition is handed down to us. At the same time, it also starts with us. Our obligation is clear: We must strive to do our very best, to challenge ourselves. Then we can expect no less from our children.

On this day, I will take five minutes to rededicate myself to the vision and tenacity it takes to create a better world for a future generation of blacks in America and around the world.

October 12

CRITICISM

Before healing others, heal thyself.
—WOLOF *proverb*

We're usually ready to donate advice. We listen to our friend's problem and it doesn't seem difficult to dispense an instant prescription. But when it comes to our own problems, we often don't have a clue. How can we be so knowing in the one instance, and so slow-witted or unsure in the other?

Let's make certain our own houses are in order before pointing out the dust balls elsewhere. Perhaps the trait that irritates us about our spouse or lover is one we're afraid to acknowledge in ourselves. None of us is perfect, and none of us needs to be a perfectionist in order to be a decent, warm soul. We can learn to be critical of ourselves without being caustic or self-loathing.

On this day, I will take five minutes to reflect upon an attitude of mine that may be making the completion of one of my goals difficult or impossible. Having done that, I pledge to work through that attitude so that I will accomplish my goal.

October 13

OPTIMISM

My idea of life is to forget the bad and live for the good there is in it. This is my motto.

—SQUIRE DOWD

When bad things happen to us, it is often difficult to let them go, particularly if the evil was prolonged, as in, say, a childhood of abuse or negligence. Even single incidents can linger on in our memories, stirring anger and perhaps confirming our belief that life is unfair or filled with disappointments.

Obsession with past wrongs—and even our own failures—can work for or against us. Yes, it can cripple us, it can bring us down and hold us there. It can also drive us to work harder, to be a better parent than our own, to channel our efforts to help others, to end poverty, to change laws, or run for office. Seeing the good in life enables us to do these things. Let's acknowledge the good and live for it, and search for it always.

At the end of this day, I will take five minutes to find at least one good thing that happened to me, no matter how small.

WORK

I go fur adgitatin'. But I believe dere is works belongs wid adgitatin', too.

—SOJOURNER TRUTH

We have found that it is sometimes necessary to plan protest marches, file law suits, and make our voices heard loudly and clearly when things are unjust. On a personal level, each of us knows when he or she needs to make a stand.

But all our agitating is for naught if we are not prepared to utilize the opportunities resulting from it. To vote, we need to study the candidates and the issues. To work, we need the relevant education or training. This requires agitating. *Yourself.*

On this day, I will do at least one concrete thing that will advance me toward my goal.

October 15

GRIEF

A month after her death, I found the courage to sleep in Mama's bed. I wanted to feel her spirit, even prayed, insane woman that I had become, for an apparition or a voice. . . . I felt nothing except pain.

—GLORIA WADE-GAYLES

After the death of a loved one, it may seem the hardest thing to carry on, to put our lives back together. We've got to allow ourselves the time to grieve before we can think about tomorrow.

There are all kinds of grief in life; we can't really practice it in order to lessen it. But we can allow grief its time, and know that, as bereft as we feel, we will heal.

On this day, I will take five minutes to meditate upon God, the mysterious life-force, or my personal inner strength—whatever it is that gives me the strength to cope with life's crises.

October 16

EMOTION

*Emotion is what makes me what I am today.
It makes me play bigger than I am.*

—CHARLES BARKLEY

We can spend an awful lot of time denying our emotions, stifling our emotions, and fighting our emotions. In our society, emotion has come to take on a negative meaning, as something that reduces us or limits us. We learn very early how to hide or suppress our feelings for fear of anyone using them to belittle us.

What a shame we have cramped ourselves this way. Emotion can fuel us, giving us the power and stamina to persevere and to fight for what we want.

We are emotional beings; let's put all parts of ourselves to work.

On this day, I will take five minutes to remember when I was angered or upset, and I will imagine that emotion as fueling me toward my goal.

PERSUASIVENESS

If there's one thing I know, it's how to sell the show.
—MUHAMMAD ALI

Muhammad Ali had what it takes to draw people to the ring—the talent, the style, the handsome looks. But one thing more separated him from all the other heavyweight champions—he knew he had to sell the show, and the "show" was Ali! His mixture of flamboyance, audacity, and the ability to articulate and provoke drew the cameras and mikes to him, and the world always wanted to watch and listen.

We may feel reticent or have doubts about our charisma factor, but we *can* surmount this. Whatever the product we have to sell—whether ourselves, our services, a thing, or an idea—we need to project and to be articulate in our pitch. We must summon up our natural enthusiasm for what we're selling and persuade through confidence in ourselves or our argument.

On this day, I will take five minutes to remember a time when I was masterful at making an impression at a job interview, a school interview, or athletic tryout.

OPTIMISM

It's easy 'nough to titter w'en de stew is
*   smokin' hot,*
But hit's mighty ha'd to giggle
*   w'en de's nuffin' in de pot.*
  —PAUL LAURENCE DUNBAR, *from "Philosophy"*

It's easy to keep our spirits up when things are chug-
ging along according to plan, but how do we maintain our equilibrium when setbacks and slowdowns
threaten our dreams and challenge our souls? These
times when we are most tested are occasions for us
to reach deep down into ourselves, to our spiritual
core. Perhaps it is our belief in God that restores us;
perhaps it is our own well of inner strength. We may
decide to redouble our efforts; then again, it may be
all we can do just to hang on.

It may inspire us to know that there are many
who reach bottom before working their way to the top.
If we make it a habit to visualize success at whatever
we attempt, the images we conjure can strengthen us
during our bleaker moments.

On this day, I will take five minutes to visualize
myself achieving my goals.

RELATIONSHIPS

Never follow a beast into its lair.
—CHUANA proverb

There are some people who are just plain no good for us. They include those who are physically and/or verbally abusive and those with addictions to drugs or alcohol. These folks need professional help and must themselves possess the ability to recognize their problem and the desire to change.

But beyond the obviously troubled individuals just mentioned, we must also be cautious about the people who can bring us down with their pessimism, their unfocused anger, their self-obsession, or their extreme possessiveness.

There are beasts, big and small, around us. Let's think twice before we accept their invitations to visit their lairs. It may not be so easy to get out.

On this day, I will take five minutes to reflect upon my personal relationships, especially any that seem psychically draining. I pledge to end or modify those relationships so that they are less of a weight.

October 20

RELAXATION

The most important part of good health and relief from stress is surrounding yourself with people who love you.

—WILMA RUDOLPH

Spending time with people we love and enjoy being with can do wonders for our spirits. African-Americans have always understood this. When we relax, kick back, laugh and party, our troubles seem to disappear. It might be a temporary means of stress reduction, but the good feelings that carry over into the next day at work can help put things into perspective.

Knowing we have a safety net of sanity, support, and love makes life more precious and our blues more tolerable.

Let's make time for good times.

On this day, I pledge to find time to get together with friends or family members, or at least to call them.

October 21

WILL/COURAGE

Behind each act of courage you will find an unbreakable will.

—Overheard in a Detroit office

The battles are not really with others, but with ourselves. We must fortify our willpower to give us the confidence to stay strong. How do we develop this willpower? By daily affirmations of our ability to accomplish anything we put our minds to; and by daily putting our shoulders to the task of making our dreams realities.

On this day I will do at least one concrete thing that will advance me toward one of my goals.

October 22

NATIONALISM

*The nationalist space is a womb space, where
you can be nurtured in a positive way. But you
don't live in a womb. Babies who aren't born, die.*
— BERNICE JOHNSON REAGON

Developing from a base—a strong, personal, ethnic
foundation—affords us knowledge of ourselves and
our people.

But if were all to refuse to interact with whites,
we would give them total power to make laws for us
and policy decisions that affect us, to define American art and thought, and to enforce these notions
in our education and national belief systems. We
need to assert and uphold our culture and perspective, which we do when we *venture out* with a strong
ethnic identity.

*On this day, I will take five minutes to meditate
upon something I have that reminds me of my
African descent and let it inspire me to do the best I
can in whatever I have to accomplish.*

October 23

PREPAREDNESS/RECEPTIVITY

Before eating, open thy mouth.

—*WOLOF proverb*

When we sit down at the table, we must prepare ourselves to receive nourishment. We must lift our forks, open our mouths, and follow through. Hunger, or appetite, brings us to the table in the first place.

So it goes in life. There are many possibilities for enrichment as long as we are receptive to them. We are foolish not to accept help when it is offered. We must keep our eyes open for opportunities; they are there, and if we pass them by, someone else will come along to claim them.

The world is a banquet table for me to feast at. On this day, I will take a bite and savor it.

October 24

WORK

I learned that no matter what you may or may not have, as perceived by a misguided community about what is valuable, people understand hard work and talent—and it can prevail.

—MAXINE WATERS

In *Children of the Dream*, Maxine Waters talked of growing up dark-skinned in a community that prized light skin and straight hair. Still, there were enough neighbors who recognized Waters's talent and industriousness and gave the future state assemblywoman from Los Angeles encouragement.

There are all sorts of ways we might not live up to the expectations of others. We can go crazy worrying about the ways we don't fit in, or we can concentrate on getting the work done.

On this day, I will remember that we are all so different in so many ways, and I will take five minutes to visualize putting my talents to work and imagine that my efforts are successful.

October 25

SELF-MOTIVATION

*I came out of the sixties, when people had
commitment and passion, and when there was
aliveness and purpose.*

—BARBARA ANN TEER

How sad when we wait for a "movement" to move
us! Of course we are inspired when we are surrounded by energy and passion. That kind of drive
feeds on itself. When everyone brings his own flame
to the fire it grows brighter and stronger so that more
and more are illuminated by it and drawn to it.

While it *appears* that African-American activ-
ism has been rekindled, we don't know how strong
it will be or how long it will continue. We have to
make our own commitment, but we can also enlist
the support of our family and friends to make our
own mini-movement. Let's make sure to keep our
own passion and purpose strong and not wait till it
is fashionable to do so.

*On this day, I will take five minutes to do one thing
that either helps toward the empowerment of black
people or advances me further toward the
accomplishment of one of my goals.*

HURRYING

Haste has no blessing.

—*SWAHILI proverb*

Most of our life, it seems, is spent in slow motion. Things never seem to come quickly enough—good things, that is. Our elders tell us, "Be patient." Everyone else echoes the sentiment. So we tend to do the opposite—and rush into things.

There are times to be patient and times to hurry. The important thing is to know when to do what.

On this day, I will take five minutes to remember that there is nothing to be gained by being frantic and hurried.

October 27

THINKING

Nothing pains some people more than having to think.

—MARTIN LUTHER KING, JR.

People who exercise their minds all the time will certainly find it less strenuous than those who prefer living without thought. Like a weekend athlete who huffs and pants on the tennis court or baseball diamond, the reluctant thinker, when called upon to use his brain, will find the whole process exhausting and fall far short of his potential.

We must never fail to stretch our minds. Without questioning, we do not progress. Without debate, we do not grow.

On this day, I pledge to read one chapter of a book or the front-page items of the newspaper, or watch the television news, all with a pad and pencil in hand. I will jot down questions and incongruities about what I am reading or watching.

October 28

WISDOM

*Wisdom is greater than knowledge, for wisdom
includes knowledge and the due use of it.*
—JOSEPH SEVELLI CAPPONI

Knowledge, by itself, is not enough. We can have a
firm grasp of all the facts in libraries of books, we
can sit through the lectures of learned men and
women, but if all that information isn't processed in
ways to enhance our lives, we are not much more
than trivia experts.

Today, African-Americans, as agitators and
educators alike, are helping change the things our
children learn at school. As multicultural education
represents us more fairly, we must make it do more
than simply inform. We must make it inspire. That
is wisdom—using knowledge, applying it, making it
work for us.

*On this day, I will take five minutes to look for a
piece of information that will help me toward
accomplishing one of my goals.*

October 29

SELF-DETERMINATION

If I didn't define myself for myself, I would be crunched into other people's fantasies for me and eaten alive.

—AUDRE LORDE

Mother may have fantasized a doctor. Dad may have fantasized a business tycoon. Our spouse may have had another idea in mind. When we try to live up to others' expectations, we surrender our own. Our career, mates, life-style, political and religious beliefs are all up for grabs.

It seems incredible that this can happen; it does. Let's not become another casualty. We need to examine our own wants and needs and pursue our heart's desires. It's our life; let others fantasize for themselves.

On this day, I will take five minutes to be quiet, listen to my inner self, and determine who I am and what I should be.

HERITAGE

*What all achieving blacks successfully do is turn
the color of black into the color of victory.*
    —*AUDREY EDWARDS and CRAIG K. POLITE,
    from* Children of the Dream

In our society, being black has so often been seen as being lazy, stupid, or irresponsible. Yes, *we* know that's not who we are. Unfortunately, there are some of us who have come to believe all the worst stereotypes.

We need to do what Kwanzaa founder Maulana Karenga suggests and take the highest ideals of our culture and live up to them. To be black is to be successful, responsible, industrious, creative, and full of hope and faith. Knowledge of our heritage makes us realize that black is, was, and will continue to be the color of victory.

*On this day, I will take five minutes to meditate
upon something I have that reminds me of my
African descent—it may be a piece of African cloth, a
sculpture, a family photograph—and let it inspire me
to do the best I can in whatever I have to accomplish
today.*

October 31

ABILITY

Before we were allowed to play basketball, we were told we didn't have the ability. Before we were allowed to box, we were told we didn't have the ability.

—ERIC V. COPAGE

There have been similar notions espoused about the abilities of black athletes as pitchers and quarterbacks. It should teach us that we should never allow others to psych us out, never allow others to define or limit our abilities.

We should also gain confidence that any one of us can excel in the area of our interest, and that as a group, African-Americans can dominate any field.

On this day, I will take five minutes to visualize myself excelling at my job or my studies.

November 1

FLEXIBILITY

Always have more than one iron in the fire.

—Common saying overheard in a
New York City office

There's always a risk that a particular project or prospect won't play out to our satisfaction. The chance of failure should not discourage us, but let's recognize how important it is to have a number of things percolating.

When we expand our opportunities, the death of one does not deal us a fatal blow.

On this day, in addition to my main goal, I will spend five minutes and think of at least two more goals and ways to accomplish them.

November 2

PLAY

*I do work very hard, and when I finish a
project, I can party all night. Or I can be
happy going somewhere very quiet with my kids
and digging holes in the sand.*

—DEBBIE ALLEN

Finding balance in one's life can be tricky. Some of
us feel guilty or antsy when we're not working. We
undervalue play; after all, hard work is rewarded (with
promotions, raises, bonuses), but no one tells us to
keep up the good play. Digging holes in the sand
with our children allows us to unwind and share intimate moments that we may all treasure for a lifetime. Exercise and relaxation help to combat stress.
Having a good time with our spouse or lover can
cement the bond between us, which we must do if
we're going to have a sturdy enough relationship to
make it through the difficult moments.

Let's be sure to leave room on our calendars
for play.

*On this day, I will take five minutes to list five non-
business, non-job-related activities that are important
to me. And I will pledge to leave room for them in my
life.*

PRIVACY

There comes a point when you really have to
spend time with yourself to know who you are.
Black people need to be with ourselves.

—BERNICE JOHNSON REAGON

As individuals, we need to know, understand, and love ourselves. As a people, we also need to know, understand, and love ourselves. We do this—privately, intimately, and socially—in our homes, in our art, and throughout the collective celebration of our heritage at Kwanzaa.

We've probably all experienced those moments of decompression and relief when we can be together after our dealings with an often insensitive, if not egregiously ornery, world. We can be grateful for those times and look forward to them, as they enable us to get in touch with parts of ourselves.

On this day, I will choose one likely person and begin
the long process of forging an alliance based on trust.
Or I will suggest to someone I am beginning to trust
that we get together over coffee.

November 4

DREAMS

It's time to move from hope to making what we hoped about and dreamed about real. Now is the time for the prophecy to be fulfilled.
—CALVIN O. BUTTS

Can any one of us be content with only his dreams? Hardly. Hopes and dreams give us reason to live and struggle, but should never replace solid action. To visualize success is one thing; to live it, another.

We must use our dreams to drive us, to make us work. Only then can we hope to achieve. Realizing our dreams gives us the confidence to dream more and bigger dreams. And why not? Why put limits on the number and breadth of our achievements? Our work is not for our glory alone, but aids and inspires our people, too. Opening five supermarkets instead of one puts five times as many people to work. It is our accomplishments as writers, architects, teachers, doctors, and designers—and yes, as parents also— that inspire others, not our mere dreams. Anyone can dream; all of us must accomplish:

On this day, I will do at least one thing that will help me accomplish one of my goals.

November 5

INDIVIDUALITY

"Young ladies don't wear shorts when they go down the road." Grandma uttered this gravely, without the least hint of a smile.
—BEBE MOORE CAMPBELL, *from* Sweet Summer

And big boys don't cry, real men don't change diapers, real women don't opt for life without children, and real African-Americans aren't Republicans. We can get pretty judgmental when others fail to meet our criteria for acceptable behavior.

When we regard the life-styles and choices of our friends, family, and peers, let us also employ the maxim of "different strokes for different folks." Of course, abusive or self-destructive behavior need not be condoned or tolerated. Still, we free ourselves when we understand that standards are seldom standard.

On this day, I will reflect upon a woman I know or a man I know. Then I will take five minutes to note qualities that are unique to him or her or different from the stereotypical image of that kind of person.

SAVORING

Exhaust the little moment.
—GWENDOLYN BROOKS

Our moments slip away. They are little moments, we think, and it's not so very tragic when they go. We waste them today and determine to be more industrious or to enjoy them more tomorrow. How much time do we lose like this?

Our moments need not be a furious blur of activity to be well lived. We can learn to find joy and contentment in ordinary events—not rushing through them with an eye to completing our tasks, but trying to appreciate them and tuning in to their simple beauty: contemplating the sunset or watching our child in her bubble bath. Let's be more sensually oriented when we are tearing the lettuce for our salads or rolling our biscuits. Maybe we can take our newspaper and coffee out to a park bench in the morning for a few minutes before work or chores.

On this day, I will try to get more out of my moments by being more keenly aware of them. I will slow down to appreciate them and ask myself how I can make them more pleasant and special.

ORIGINALITY

In search of my mother's garden, I found my own.
—ALICE WALKER

Mother and daughter, father and son—we are very different people indeed. We, the children, may be inspired by our parents' example or wish to emulate their character. But we have different strengths and passions; also, different challenges and weakness. Some beautiful specimens, as well as undesirable weeds, that grew in their gardens may sprout in ours as well. Yet our garden will be uniquely ours.

In our mother's (or father's) garden may grow tarragon and rosemary; while in ours grow basil and coriander. In place of daffodils grow tulips. In place of mustard greens grow collards. Our gardens, of course, are our lives. Perhaps ours is sprawling and lush while our mother's is confined and in neat rows. There is beauty in both.

On this day, I will take five minutes to visualize my "garden"—the good things I am trying to accomplish in my life.

November 8

AUTHENTICITY

*The varieties of human choice and thought are
not very willingly accepted when the subject is
Afro-Americans.*

—STANLEY CROUCH

We should not allow ourselves to be hampered by
some myth about what it means to be authentically
black. Did Charlie Parker, when he first picked up a
sax, say, "This instrument was invented by a dead
white man, so I'm not going to touch it"?

We are African-Americans and we should affirm this with a knowledge of our heritage and by
excelling in everything we do. We should also remember that we are human and heir to all things
human.

Our world is rich and we ought not deny ourselves a sampling of all the experiences that it has to
offer.

*On this day, I will take five minutes to meditate
upon the fact that everything—from Tibetan prayer
wheels to Irish step dancing to Delta blues to T'ang
pottery—is part of my heritage.*

November 9

PARENTHOOD

*I had . . . found that motherhood was a
profession by itself, just like schoolteaching and
lecturing.*

—IDA B. WELLS

We are competing against people of all ethnicities
for whom parenthood is a serious commitment.
These are parents who devote their time and energy
to stimulating and enriching their progeny by every
means possible.

One day our children will compete with theirs.
Let us now do all we can to prepare them. We can
encourage their interests, push them gently to explore their talents and to learn, whatever our circumstances.

*On this day, I pledge to take advantage of all that is
available—child-development books, libraries, free or
inexpensive classes for parents. On this day, I will
also pledge to attend to my children's nutritional
needs and, most of all, to praise them frequently and
love them unconditionally.*

November 10

PATRIOTISM

The fact is that blacks are not outside the American mainstream but, in [Ralph] Ellison's words, have always been "one of its major tributaries."

—CLAUDE M. STEELE

The way we've been taught, we might get the impression that our people haven't contributed much of anything to this country. But African-Americans should know we've had a broad influence here. Music, science, dance, industry, sports, and literature are just a few of the areas where we have put our stamp.

It's important for us to remember and to pass on to our children that African-Americans are essential to the definition of America. We cannot allow ourselves to be misled into thinking that all that is good about our country came via Europe.

On this day, I will take five minutes to meditate upon how African-Americans in general, and my family in particular, have helped build America.

November 11

SUCCESS

*If you can somehow think and dream of
success in small steps, every time you make a
step, every time you accomplish a small goal, it
gives you confidence to go on from there.*

—JOHN H. JOHNSON

When we visualize success, we usually think about
the end product, with an image in our heads of being
handed an Oscar or presiding over a phalanx of ex-
ecutives at a long mahogany table. While it helps to
see ourselves as successful, our images can sometimes
seem far away. We risk becoming frustrated and disillusioned, which could slow our progress or make us
give up on our dreams.

Success, or achievement, is never a one-step
deal. By mapping out the route we need to take, we
can break it down into individual steps, which will
bring us gratification all along the way to our ultimate goal. Achieving these small goals proves that
we have what it takes. Confidence builds slowly with
daily reinforcement.

*On this day, I will do something that brings me
closer to reaching one of my goals.*

November 12

SELF-PRAISE

You have to know that your real home is within.
—QUINCY JONES

It's amazing how fragile human beings can be. If we gain a few pounds, we kick ourselves. If we decide we have faltered in our careers, we grieve over having let ourselves down. If we say something silly, we brood over our "stupidity" for days. We might send ourselves negative messages constantly; how many positive ones do we send?

Every one of us needs a heavy dose of self-love in order to survive. When we love ourselves, we are comfortable within ourselves; we can forgive and accept ourselves.

We don't get praised much in life, so we must learn to do it ourselves. Learning to pat ourselves on the back can get us in the habit of focusing on our positive feelings. If we're not happy in our homes within, there's nowhere else for us to go!

On this day, I will take five minutes to meditate on five praiseworthy things about myself.

November 13

COLLECTIVE RESPONSIBILITY

We do not live for ourselves only, but for our wives and children, who are as dear to us as those of any other men.

—ABRAHAM

We live, not as hermits, untouched by others, but in families and communities.

"It's my life," you insist. Of course. Ultimately, only you can decide what is best for you. But every choice affects the lives of those around you now and those who will surround you later. Living up to your responsibilities, being active participants in life, gives incalculable rewards and considerable potential for enriching your community.

On this day, I will spend five minutes remembering a time when I was an active participant in the community, a time when I worked for the future and not just the present. I will vow to repeat and expand my participation.

SKILLS

I don't believe that you have to be mean to be successful in the ring. I don't understand why some boxers are motivated by hate. The way I see it, it's possible to be a good boxer and a good person at the same time.

—EVANDER HOLYFIELD

Perhaps we're under the impression that the ones who "make it" in life are the ones driven by anger or hatred or some "nasty streak" that compels them to acquire power. If we find no meanness inside ourselves, can we compete against individuals who seemingly possess no scruples, no shame, no heart?

Like any champion, we must be vigilant in our training and derive pride from our performance. Motivation born out of the goodness in our hearts can be as powerful as any born out of evil, and in that we must have faith.

On this day, while I am working at my job, taking care of my children, or studying, I will remember that I can be good and do well.

November 15

MIND POWER

There is a way to provide against the onslaught of poverty. It is the recognition of the power of the mind.

—A. G. GASTON

We spend the better part of our youth loading up our minds on facts and figures, very often just so we can make the grades that we think will somehow ensure a life of promise for ourselves at the end of our formal education. While we may be full of hope for our future, we've probably neglected to train our minds to ace the make-or-break mental tests that await us.

It takes as much discipline to see ourselves as successful as it does to pass those school exams we cram for. It takes developing our will to persevere, to find creative means to vault our obstacles, and to maintain both our courage and our endurance for the fight of our lives.

On this day, I will take five minutes to relax and visualize myself accomplishing one of my goals.

November 16

ROLE MODELS

*Teddy [Roosevelt] was very close to me because
we both had asthma and would stay awake at
night with our back propped up by a pillow.
But he overcame it, went to Harvard and
became a great speaker. So I decided I had to
go to Harvard, too, although at eight I didn't
know exactly what it was.*

—CORNELL WEST

Inspiration can come from many sources—our parents, teachers, elder siblings, historical figures, and contemporary role models. It may seem incongruous that something about the life of Theodore Roosevelt would resonate with a youngster from a working-class black neighborhood. But why not? It benefits us to open ourselves up to the wisdom and examples of others, no matter their ethnicity, gender, or time in history.

*On this day, I pledge to keep my mind open to all
that might help and inspire me to accomplish my
goals, regardless of the race, gender, age, or sexual
orientation from which the help or inspiration might
come.*

November 17

DISCOURAGEMENT

Black people told me, "Yo, baby, you're black.
This is America, still the white man's country.
Forget it."

—ARSENIO HALL

Why do we sometimes tell others their dreams are not possible? It's hard enough to fight the negatives that others tell us without having to fight the negatives heaped on us by fellow African-Americans.

It is our duty to encourage each other, to say, "I know you can do it." At the very least, let us clamp our mouths on the negative warnings if we cannot find it in our hearts to cheer our brothers and sisters on. Then let us take a look at the many examples of African-Americans who shunned "reality" and achieved their dreams.

On this day, I will go up to a black person who has shared his or her ambitions with me and tell him or her that I know they can accomplish their goals.

November 18

PERSEVERANCE

Every dog has his day; there is a time for all things.
— TERENCE, *from* The Eunuch

Perseverance. It's not always easy to keep up the energy and put forth the effort. There are too many days when our goals seem maddeningly distant. We want our recognition and earthly rewards *now!*

Well, there will be a time for uncorking the champagne. But, likely as not, now is the time for learning, working, growing, contributing, reassessing, developing. Small rewards are ours consistently if we know how to recognize them.

In a larger, communal sense, we African-Americans have long been waiting for our day, our time on top. Guess what—this *is* our day. It's the only day we've got. Let's appreciate our many strengths and victories *today*. Then let's get back to the work of pursuing our goals.

On this day, if I have just accomplished a goal, I will take five minutes to congratulate myself. Otherwise, I will take one concrete action—write a letter, make a call, look up an article—to further me in one of my goals.

SUBSTANCE

I'm not a star, I'm a writer. I don't want to be a star.
—TERRY MCMILLAN

Stardom is a lure to many a young writer, actor, musician—yes, even businessperson. Perhaps we feel that the spotlight of success will brighten the dark corners of our psyche, that the adulation of many will enhance our *self*-respect.

Yet the writer who focuses on getting to the top of the best-seller list and becoming a frequent talk show guest will likely concern herself with what sells, or what image she wants to project, rather than what it is she wants to say. "Stardom" is a tricky thing—ephemeral, fleeting, subject to influences beyond our control.

It is our *work* we must dedicate ourselves to, and not the trappings of success, which are empty in themselves until we fill them with a solid core of talent and wholehearted devotion.

On this day, I will take five minutes to think about what I want to do with my life. Do I feel productive? Fulfilled? What can I do that will increase my sense of satisfaction and accomplishment?

November 20

SELFISHNESS

It is time for every one of us to roll up our sleeves and put ourselves at the top of our commitment list.

—MARIAN WRIGHT EDELMAN

Where do we currently figure on our personal commitment list? Somewhere under spouses, lovers, children, and friends? It's likely. We often get so wrapped up in the demands of others that we have no time or energy left for ourselves.

Our dreams are necessary to us and we deserve the chance to fulfill them. Perhaps our families will have to make do with frozen dinners for a while, or our mates will have to run more errands or make the kids' dental appointments. The friends we'd like to invite over may have to wait until our calendar clears.

When we need time—to write our screenplay, take a night class, read, or exercise—we've got to remind ourselves that those who love us can help.

On this day, I will indulge in something that will make me feel good or make time for something I want to do.

November 21

CRISES

In every crisis there is a message. Crises are nature's way of forcing change—breaking down old structures, shaking loose negative habits so that something new and better can take their place.

—SUSAN TAYLOR

In life, there are crises. Let's accept that. Like thunderstorms, some are scarier and more explosive than others. But we must remember that as there was peace before the storm, there will be peace after.

Crises usually seem overwhelming, since they dominate our lives for a time. Let us learn to rebound from crises stronger than before.

On this day, I will take five minutes to remember a time when I was in a crisis, and I will imagine overcoming it and, while overcoming it, being infused with greater strength, confidence, composure, and optimism that will flow out into everything I do today.

November 22

AFRICAN-AMERICANS

*I thought that this beautiful feeling I'd shared
with my immediate family was exclusive to
them. I saw instead that the black feeling—the
warmth, the love, the laughter, the spontaneity—
extended beyond my household. It was as
though my own family had just grown larger.*

—JANET JACKSON

Janet Jackson is referring to how she felt when black
students bused to the public junior high school
she attended in her predominantly Jewish neighborhood. She reports, "I'd been isolated without even
knowing it."

When you go to a party comprised mainly of
African-Americans, do you feel a sense of special
comfort—of being secure, calm, not on the
defensive?

Let's treasure our time with each other. It is
pleasurable and affirming.

*Sometime during this day—whether over breakfast
with family, lunch with co-workers, or dinner with
friends—I will simply enjoy the company of African-
Americans.*

November 23

SILENCE

Silence is a great communicator. Watch a movie and note the moments that give you the greatest insight into the characters. They are the times the characters react with their eyes, their mouths, their bodies, their whole physical beings. And when the words come out but do not jibe with the body language, which do we trust more? The body language, of course.

We need silence in our lives to think, to work, to create, and to rest. The person who never stops talking may never really say much. The household with constant noise will not be a serene place—a place in which to rest, study, reflect, and create.

On this day, I will take five minutes to silently observe my thoughts as they float by.

November 24

PRIDE

*I'm perfectly satisfied to be an American Negro,
tough as it all is.*

—*JESSIE FAUSET*

There are times when some of us are asked whether
we wouldn't prefer being called simply "doctor, architect, or quarterback" rather than "black doctor,
black architect, or black quarterback." There is no
need to retreat from our heritage. Why not embrace
it in all we are and do, and feel lucky to be able
to draw from the rich matrix of our African and
African-American history, culture, and selves?

Our culture is not limiting; let's put down the
notion of restrictions and narrow definitions of ourselves. As African-American lawyers, teachers, or bus
drivers, we partake in everything human.

*On this day, I will take five minutes to meditate on
the beauty and wonder of being of African ancestry. I
will reflect upon the unique culture and strength and
creativity of our people, and thank the powers that be
for making me one of that number.*

November 25

MUSIC

There is no such thing that all blacks have rhythm. It's not that they're born with rhythm, but in black homes you always hear music. It becomes instinctive, a lot rubs off.

—ARTHUR MITCHELL

Music goes to our roots. Generation after generation, we pass on our love affair with music. It enriches our lives in countless ways, salving our pain, adding beauty in our bleakness, stirring our emotions and driving our bodies. Music has inspired artists to paint and writers to write; it is an addiction with no harmful side effects. (Unless it's too loud!)

Our music ranges from blues to pop, jazz to gospel, rap to classical. While *we* might crave bebop and our neighbor leans to Vivaldi, we must recognize that music is in the ears of the listener. Perhaps we can expand our tastes; there is joy in discovery.

On this day, I will play one song—be it Smokey Robinson, the World Saxophone Quartet, or Youssou N'Dour, and I will carefully listen to what is happening in that piece of music.

HOPE

Hope is the pillar of the world.
—KANURI *proverb*

Hope is what makes us look forward to tomorrow. Without it, our days have little meaning, and contemplating the rest of our life can depress us enormously.

African-Americans *need* hope in a major way. Where do we get it? Within ourselves—by looking at our talents, our strengths, our ability to endure and to expect and demand better.

Our ancestors had hope in the face of great persecution. We must live up to their example. Hope, we must recognize, is not a thing in limited supply, but a renewable resource.

On this day, I will take five minutes to thank the ancestors, God, and the millions of Africans and those of African descent worldwide and throughout history who have given me a firm foundation of hope and faith upon which to build my dreams. I pledge to keep my vision strong as a foundation for future generations.

PRIDE

*Aunt Jemima is the black woman who cooked
and cleaned, struggled, brought up her own
family and a white family. And if I'm ashamed
of Aunt Jemima—her head rag, her hips, her
color—then I'm ashamed of my people.*

—MAXINE WATERS

We are the descendants of slaves. This does not diminish the value of our people. Our ancestors helped
to build this country—worked its fields, laid its rail-
way lines, fought its wars.

There was a time I would never wave the
American flag. As I got older, I realized my response
discredited the contributions of my ancestors. We
have every reason to feel proud of our heritage, in
its totality. No one can mock us when we refuse to
be mocked.

*On this day, I will take five minutes to remember the
many contributions African-Americans made to the
building of this country. And I will embrace those
contributions and proclaim my entitlement to all that
is good that this country can provide.*

November 28

AFFIRMATION

I am/I can.

—*Graffito in Harlem*

To some this graffito sounds a little *too* optimistic—a sentiment of some unworldly fool. But think about it. And look around. The happiest and most successful people are those who have this self-confidence and optimism. And if they don't, they have the courage to pretend—and to persevere.

On this day, I will take five minutes to remember a time when I succeeded at something unexpectedly.

November 29

CONFIDENCE

*If I can make you think I'm King Kong, I've
won the match.*

—LYNETTE LOVE

Mental intimidation may not seem as necessary to
us as it is to Tae Kwan Do Olympic Gold Medalist
Lynette Love, who is also given to smiling during
matches to manage tension and rattle her opponents.
But an aura of self-confidence can serve us as well
in our workaday world.

*On this day, I will take the time to note my positive
qualities and successes, and will focus the good feeling
I get on a strategy to achieve one of my goals.*

November 30

ORIGINALITY

*I decided, if I'm going to be poor and black
and all, the least thing I'm going to do is try
and find out who I am. I created everything
about me.*

—ORNETTE COLEMAN

We are all our own creations. Some of us may create
ourselves in response to others' demands and expectations,
while some may purposefully fly in the face
of outside influences to seek out our individual style.
There may be safety in following the dictates of the
majority—there is certainly less ridicule and less to
fight—but there is greater joy in finding our own
style, our own voice.

*On this day, I pledge to pay attention to myself—the
way I dress, the way I decorate my apartment, the
way I think—and take special delight in how I do
what I do.*

December 1

FEELING

Man, if you gotta ask, you'll never know.
—LOUIS ARMSTRONG

Armstrong was responding to someone asking him what jazz was. Indeed, *some* things just can't be explained.

Understanding ourselves and our world is important, no argument there. But there are times we've got to go with the feeling. If a special someone is nibbling our ear in an especially delicious way, do we really need to volunteer, "You know, I enjoy the way your breath feels on that little space behind the . . . blah, blah, blah"? Our special someone is likely to recoil in shock. We can get the same point across just by going, "Mmmmmmmm."

I trust my intuition, and on this day, I will be especially attuned to its working.

December 2

ACCEPTANCE

*Start with what you know and build on what
you have.*

—KWAME NKRUMAH

We are who we are and we must build from there.
Depending on our ambitions, this can be distressing.
But there are inspiring examples of self-made suc-
cesses, people who began with less than we have.
Hard work, perseverance, and sheer will can work
miracles.

Remember, too, that we are part of a collective
enterprise. Even if we do not go as far as we'd like,
those who follow us, by standing on our shoulders,
will have a shorter climb to make.

*On this day, I pledge to do at least one thing that
advances me toward one of my goals.*

December 3

FULFILLMENT

I find, in being black, a thing of beauty: a joy;
a strength; a secret cup of gladness.

—OSSIE DAVIS, from Purlie Victorious

There are times we sing our blues. And we know that society in general often sees us as handicapped. Yes, we have known suffering; yet despite our suffering—perhaps because of it—we have found in ourselves a wellspring of joy. To be black is to be triumphant, to be strong, to be jubilant. We know love, beauty, exuberance, and poetry.

Let's make it a habit to take stock of our heritage and let our specialness become our own secret cup of gladness.

On this day, I will take five minutes to meditate
upon something I have that reminds me of my
African descent—it may be a piece of African cloth, a
sculpture, a family photograph, a quote from Malcolm
X—and let it inspire me to do the best I can in
whatever I have to accomplish.

December 4

VANITY

Vanity is the beginning of corruption.
—JOAQUIM MARIA MACHADO DE ASSÍS

A certain degree of vanity is seen as healthy. It implies we are proud of ourselves. But vanity can be our ruination if, self-satisfied, we allow our drive to accomplish things to be slowed or stalled. Too much time spent solely on touting our beauty, our strength, or our talents leaves less time to put our abilities to good use.

Flattery can become addictive. And when we can be flattered, we can often be bought. Flattery opens us up to the machinations of others who would like to weaken us. We stop working, even for ourselves, because, after all, *we* know how great we are.

"Mirror time" serves a purpose. We African-Americans, in particular, hear too many negatives and not enough compliments. But taking time to appreciate ourselves should inspire us to put down the mirror and take care of business.

On this day, I will remember to embrace the compliments that come my way, but I will not become entangled in them.

December 5

DESPAIR

After distress, solace.

—*SWAHILI proverb*

Sometimes, in our efforts to move through life with courage and fortitude, we deny ourselves the right to show any emotion that might render us less than stoic. Yet when we experience great loss or disappointment, it is natural to grieve. We lose no dignity by showing our despair or sadness. Men, in particular, need to understand this. We need to release our anguish. Why not allow our friends and loved ones to help us? It's okay to seek consolation; it's okay if we need to be held.

On this day, I will take five minutes to recognize that crying is healthy, and that holding it in can do damage. And if, in the course of this meditation, I remember a time when I wish I could have cried, I will give myself permission to cry at last.

December 6

GRACEFULNESS

My whole nation is graceful. Nobody has to tell us how to walk or how to stand. We have an air, a dignity: Whatever happens, you keep your head up.

—*IMAN*

Not all of us can make a claim to gracefulness, yet we know it when we see it. Gracefulness is an ease in motion that suggests inner composure and poise. It is not forced or stiff, but natural in feel and seemingly effortless.

There are moments of gracefulness in all our lives that we may not have named as such. Graceful might in fact be the way we react to defeat or disappointments, or the way we respond to crises. It is the finesse with which we get through our challenges.

On this day, I will take five minutes to remember a time when I was in a crisis. I will imagine myself responding calmly and efficiently, letting all my anxiety and worry flow into solving the problem at hand.

December 7

FULFILLMENT

I don't think there's anything in the world I can't do. . . . In my creative source, whatever that is, I don't see why I can't sculpt. Why shouldn't I? Human beings sculpt. I'm a human being.

—MAYA ANGELOU

We spend a lot of time thinking "I could never do that." Even when it's not a conscious thought, we may swiftly dismiss or refuse to consider opportunities for expression and fulfillment. Why can't we learn to play chess, fly an airplane, go kayaking, or, for that matter, start a new career or rise in our chosen profession?

In deciding where we want to take our lives, let's remember that no trail is off-limits to us.

On this day, I will consider what might make my life fuller or more interesting. And I pledge to follow up my desire with action.

December 8

CHALLENGES

She was very stern and very firm. She pushed me, and I didn't like it for a long time. But now I push myself, because I know that my limits are more than I thought they were.

—YASMEEN GRAHAM

Perhaps we can recall a person in our life who was exceptionally tough on us. We might have hated them, or resented their attention, but now we can look back and see that they actually pushed us further than we ourselves thought we could go.

James Comer, a Yale psychiatrist who works with inner-city children, found that programs that challenged kids instead of coddling them had better results.

Let's not be afraid to challenge lovingly those around us, and to accept challenges from them.

On this day, I will take five minutes to visualize a friend, colleague, coach, or relative pushing me to help me live up to my full potential in achieving one of my goals.

December 9

LOOKING BACK

The underdog does not stop to philosophize about his position.

PAUL LAURENCE DUNBAR, *from* The Fanatics

While we can use our time-outs to correct our mistakes or to put in place a new strategy for the play ahead, we need to focus our energy on trying to move on, to break out from behind.

Again, this is *not* to say we shouldn't occasionally glance at the clock and get an idea of our position. The point is this: If we dwell on poor past performance—individually or as a team—we risk psyching ourselves out, demoralizing ourselves, and wasting time better spent maneuvering into the lead.

On this day, I will do at least one thing that advances me toward my goal.

December 10

SELF-HELP

Solve your own problem by curing your own defects.
—JOSEPH SEVELLI CAPPONI

Quite often we are directly responsible for the very problems we face. Our cynicism dampens our career. Our alcoholism ruins our marriage. Our tempers destroy friendships, and our pride keeps us from getting the help we need. There are measures we can take. We need to assess our problems and look at how we might be contributing to them. Then we can take action.

Sometimes, however, the problem is not one of our own making. When such a problem doesn't go away, we must consider our options. We can leave or fight it. The defect is not always ours, but it is up to us to discern which ones are—and which are not.

On this day, I will take five minutes to focus on something I do that I know I shouldn't do, and I will take one step toward changing it.

December 11

BIGOTRY

I grew up hearing about the ways black people were abused, but we were also told we were much better in many ways than the people who were doing this. We just absolutely did not understand why white people had to be so contrary.

—BERNICE JOHNSON REAGON

While other ethnicities in our country may have it rough, there seems nothing like the animosity toward our people. But we cannot sit around trying to puzzle it out. Nor can we waste time lamenting the situation. Rather, we need to use the heat of prejudice to solder our resolve to triumph. It should drive us to strengthen ourselves, through individual and collective effort.

On this day, I will choose one likely person, and begin the long process of forging an alliance based on trust. Or I will suggest to someone I am beginning to trust that we get together over coffee.

December 12

COMPASSION

*Make some muscle in your head,
but use the muscle in your heart.*

—IMAMU AMIRI BARAKA

Our hearts allow us to take things beyond the obvious into consideration. We are sometimes nagged by a little voice that cries, "Don't be soft," yet occasional softness needn't be a character flaw; it can be a virtue. When we permit our hearts to have a say in our decisions, we are guided by compassion.

By all means, use your head; it's there to sort things out and make rational choices. But let's make room for our hearts, too, which can show us the better way.

*On this day, I will remember a time when I was
compassionate or forgiving.*

ACCOMPLISHMENT

You can't hang around bathing your body in the reflection of a trophy

—BILL COSBY

It is indeed wonderful to have our moments of glory. We should enjoy them to the fullest. No doubt we've worked hard and have earned our rewards. But then we need to move on, or else a decade from now we'll still be bragging about our ten-year-old accomplishment.

The joy, after all, should come largely from the act of working toward the goal and the excitement as we move closer to it—not from those few hours we are being feted.

Let's put the trophy in the trophy case.

On this day, I will take five minutes to appreciate my past successes and allow them to motivate me to work toward my next goal.

December 14

ADVISERS

I have wise advisers . . . and I ask them, "Are my goals realistic? Am I moving in a good direction?" Even though I'm the one who finally decides . . . I require a wide range of opinion.
—JANET JACKSON

Gathering the advice and expertise of others can help us see things in ways we hadn't considered before.

If our bank account allows, we can buy advice from doctors, nutritionists, therapists, career counselors, money advisers. If our means are more restricted, let's take advantage of all the teachers, clergy, professional organizations, adult classes, and mentors available to us. Our resources are more abundant than they may appear.

On this day, I will take five minutes to concentrate on one of my goals, and I will write down three sources—people, publications, or institutions, for instance—where I might get advice as to how best to accomplish my goal.

December 15

LOVE

Love is mutually feeding each other, not one living on another like a ghoul.

—BESSIE HEAD

Romantic love flourishes with mutual respect, which, in turn, is engendered by a commitment by both to nourish the relationship and each other. Yes, duty plays a part in love, as unromantic as that may sound, but it is a duty that is lovingly and cheerfully borne.

There may be times when, by necessity, one partner takes charge of a specific aspect of the relationship, but the contributions of each should balance out over time. We need to consider our relationships continually, and make sure we are doing our part to nourish them so they thrive.

On this day, I will do for my mate, best friend, or close relative something thoughtful that he or she usually does for me.

December 16

ACCOMPLISHMENT

People will know you're serious when you produce.
—MUHAMMAD ALI

▰▰▰▰

What Muhammad Ali produced was knockouts. Anyone stepping into the ring with him knew he was serious.

When we produce, we go beyond words. After a time, promises and declarations sound hollow and silly, even to our own ears.

"I am the greatest" would have made us laugh had Ali never won a fight. Having results to show is proof for ourselves. The results needn't be the end product, either. If we desire to start up our own business, we show we are serious when we take a night class in Small Business Start-ups, or spend time studying the trade magazines that pertain to our field, or moonlight to acquire the capital we need. When we hang up our shingle, we let the *world* know how serious we are!

On this day, I will take another step toward accomplishing my goal.

BEGINNINGS

A forest that has sheltered you, you should not call a patch of scrub.

—*Oji proverb*

As we make progress in our lives, we may want to erase the memory of our beginnings. Perhaps we despise the backward town where we grew up, the suburb that offered nothing but boredom, or the overcrowded housing project that endangered us and denied us freedom. We may never want to return to *that place;* nevertheless, that is the place where we became who we are.

We can come to accord that place some respect, then, when we acknowledge that it spawned us, our hopes and ambitions unchecked. With time, we may begin to see that there were a lot of people there doing the best they could. We see that narrow minds and low expectations are not indigenous to any one location. Nor are hope and effort and greatness.

On this day, I will take five minutes to think back to my beginnings and reflect on my growth since that time.

December 18

INTIMIDATION

*I've never learned to be afraid of people who are
more powerful than I.*

— JAMAICA KINCAID

Perhaps we would deny it, but many of us *are* intimidated by people with more power than we have; this is most noticeable in our work environment. We may fear saying something stupid or appearing uninformed or uninteresting. Possibly we decide to distance ourselves, feeling that diligence in our work is enough.

Social connections do count in most fields, however. If we want to make progress, it is wise to deal with our nervousness and make an effort to associate with those "over" us so that they can come to know us better and know what we have to offer.

*On this day, I will go up to my boss, or someone
who could help me attain my goal, and engage him or
her in a very light, very brief conversation.*

December 19

One of the recurring success themes in the African-American community is the frequency with which being a victim actually drives ambition.

—AUDREY EDWARDS and CRAIG K. POLITE, from Children of the Dream

To be African-American implies that at least once in our lives, if not over and over again, we have known the meaning of victimization. Perhaps it was when we tried to get a promotion and were held back; when we browse through certain stores and are treated like would-be thieves.

If we are angry, let's *use* that anger. The idea is to create a world where we will feel less victimized, so that generations of African-Americans to come will know victimhood less and pride more.

On this day, I will take five minutes to remember a time when I felt victimized, and I will pledge to use that memory to fuel me at work, in raising my child, or at whatever task I have before me today, so that I help create a better world for African-Americans.

December 20

HUMOR

Funny is an attitude.

—FLIP WILSON

We marvel at the quick wits of comedians and think, "I'd love to be that funny." Well, comic timing *is* something to be honed. Bill Cosby or Richard Pryor makes us howl not by mere dint of inspiration but by working at it.

That doesn't mean *we* can't be funny. All of us have an aptitude for humor, but not always the attitude. "Funny" is the way we look at the world, being able to recognize its absurdities. Funny is the ability to find the peculiarities in ourselves and hold them up for closer inspection.

At the end of this day, I will take five minutes to look at some quite ordinary occurrence that would be funny if viewed from a different perspective.

December 21

SELF-ESTEEM

*If you are not feeling good about you, what
you're wearing outside doesn't mean a thing.*

—LEONTYNE PRICE

Clothes, to many of us, can be one of life's little pleasures. No doubt about it, our spirits lift when we shed our baggy sweats and try on a beautifully cut new dress or suit.

But if we are hounded by feelings of insecurity or self-pity, no piece of apparel is going to give us more than a temporary boost. It's what's inside that needs the attention. What we admire in the mirror cannot bestow true pride in ourselves.

Let's have fun with clothes, but be serious with the needs of the heart, mind, and soul beneath them.

*On this day, I will take five minutes to reflect on one
issue that might be troubling me in my life. And then
I will come up with a plan to fix it.*

December 22

SELF-HELP

If the white man gives you anything, just remember, when he gets ready he will take it right back.

—*FANNIE LOU HAMER*

While the vote was "given" to us during Reconstruction, it was all but stripped from us during post-Reconstruction, when our ancestors were threatened with bodily harm if they voted, or were excluded by illegal "grandfather clauses," or denied participation in the process in any number of ways.

When we are "given" something, we must solidify our advances so they cannot be reappropriated. We must use our power relentlessly, and build on it so that we have leverage.

On this day, I will do something to help or give encouragement to my fellow African-Americans. I might buy a black-made product, patronize a black-owned store, or offer encouragement or help to a black person who is working on a project.

December 23

INNER PEACE

My life is actually better than it appears because of my inner peace. I used to be my own worst enemy. Bu that has changed.

—OPRAH WINFREY

An awful lot of cold and cruel notions are floating around out there. When we take them to heart and allow them to rule our minds, we cannot have peace.

When we learn to love and accept ourselves, to recognize what is true and valuable for *us*, we can reject the negatives and the hype and work toward the goals we cherish. Inner peace does not manifest itself in outer stagnation, but kindles our drive to achieve.

On this day, I will take five minutes to breathe deeply, relax, and rid myself of mental noise and stress.

December 24

FAMILY

My family has always given me a place to be,
a place to be loved in and to love.
—BILLY DEE WILLIAMS

For years we have listened to many wail about the plight of the African-American family. Perhaps we have joined the chorus ourselves.

Yet the African-American family has endured much since its unwholesome transfer to American soil. Upon emancipation, some of our ancestors journeyed thousands of miles trying to track down loved ones who had been torn from them.

In any family situation, we may get frustrated or downright crazy sometimes. We often have to pull away a bit to find out who we are, to distance ourselves from our parents' or siblings' expectations.

Yet the family remains, for most of us, our most significant means of support and sustenance. It takes work and respect to make it function for us; when it does, we are rewarded in love.

On this day, I will express my love, support, or appreciation to a family member or surrogate family member who has supported me.

December 25

UNITY

I am because we are; and since we are, therefore I am.

—JOHN MBUTI

We are not solely individuals but part of a community. Our concentric circles begin with our family, then move outward to include our neighborhood, the African-American community, the American community, and the global community.

When we make ourselves stronger, we make our African-American community stronger. When our African-American community is stronger, it makes every individual in it stronger by providing more power, more opportunities, more role models, and more hope

On this day, I will take five minutes to remember that one of the results of working so hard to attain my goals is that in attaining my goals I help empower and advance not only myself, but my family and the entire African-American community.

December 26

SELF-DETERMINATION

There are people who say I'm crazy. That's okay. I can live with that.

—CARL LEWIS

If we spend our lives worrying about what people will say, what kinds of choices are we making? Whose life are we living? It can be difficult when we desire to live up to, say, a father's or mother's image. We can confuse their wants with ours and wind up the most depressed and frustrated adult on the block.

Let them talk, whoever "they" may be. Keep in mind they've got their own motivations for saying what they do, especially when it comes to knocking our ambitions. We have to live up to ourselves—our own morals, values, and dreams—or else we end up barely living at all.

On this day, I will take five minutes and visualize that I have accomplished one of my goals

December 27

COLLECTIVE WORK
AND RESPONSIBILITY

*No matter what accomplishment you make,
somebody helps you.*

—ALTHEA GIBSON

Whatever any of us achieves, we have to credit the many people who helped us in our development: parents, grandparents, siblings, teachers, mentors, friends, and coaches. Beyond these, we must give thanks to the courageous African-Americans who lived before us, who put their lives on the line—and yes, lost them, too—so that we could be free today.

Let's be proud of our accomplishments. We work hard and deserve our recognition. Let us also remember that we might not have been able to effect them had others left the struggle to us.

*On this day, I will take five minutes to remember
when someone helped me accomplish a task, or when
I helped someone else.*

December 28

COOPERATIVE ECONOMICS

My father was the kind who would say, "If a black man opens a store, go shop in it."
—CALVIN O. BUTTS

XIIIIIIIX

We can always do more to support our people, because we all benefit when our brothers and sisters succeed. If it means going a block farther to a black-owned produce stand or shoe store, let's do it. And if the quality of the merchandise disappoints us, let's communicate that to the owner so we give her every chance to rectify the situation and count on us as a permanent customer.

Let's buy books and albums by African-Americans, and go to movies by African-American directors. Remember the saying "Put your money where your mouth is." Let's *show* support, and not decry the lack of it.

On this day, I pledge to buy at least one item from a black vendor.

December 29

PURPOSE

On the way to one's beloved, there are no hills.
—KENYAN *proverb*

Of course there are hills, sometimes mountains. But it *seems* as if there are no hills. Why? Because, like a baby driven to walk, we are undeterred by the obstacles between us and our goal.

We African-Americans have certainly had our share of disappointments and setbacks. But we have also learned that when we are really focused, *nothing* can hold us back. When we believe that our goal is worthy and that we are worthy to achieve it, we are more than halfway there. We need only plant our feet on the road and keep moving forward.

On this day, I will do at least one thing that will help me accomplish one of my goals.

December 30

CREATIVITY

I know why the caged bird sings!
—PAUL LAURENCE DUNBAR

We can all feel a bit like the caged bird at times, confined in the roles we play, expected to conform to the expectations of others.

A bird has wings to fly. Caged, it can do little more than flutter its wings in frustration. It sings to give vent to its misery, to express itself, and to create beauty for itself.

We all need to find outlets for our stifled selves. In the act of creating, we enter an almost meditative state where our troubles cease to exist and our spirit heals and fortifies.

Painting, playing an instrument, or writing a poem may readily occur to us as means of creative expression, but so are woodworking, gardening, cooking, or needlepoint—whatever appeals to our individual natures.

On this day, I will do something artfully: I will write a letter, make a pencil sketch, or just rearrange one of my rooms in a different way.

December 31

INDEX

PERMISSIONS

ABOUT THE AUTHOR

Eric V. Copage has contributed articles to the pages of *The New York Times Magazine,* where he is currently an editor. He was a staff reporter for *Life* magazine and the *New York Daily News* and a music columnist for *Essence* magazine. He has a degree in ethnomusicology and has traveled extensively in West Africa. He is the author of *Kwanzaa: An African-American Celebration of Culture and Cooking* (William Morrow, 1991).